A HIDDEN ECONOMY

A HIDDEN ECONOMY

Māori in the privatised military industry

MARIA BARGH

First published in 2015 by Huia Publishers
39 Pipitea Street, PO Box 12280
Wellington, Aotearoa New Zealand
www.huia.co.nz

ISBN 978-1-77550-197-8

Copyright © Maria Bargh 2015

Cover image © Oleg Zabielin / image ID: 203119372,
Shutterstock Images LLC

Photos courtesy of those interviewed unless otherwise indicated. The sources
are not identified to protect the confidentiality of the people involved.

This book is copyright. Apart from fair dealing for the purpose of private study,
research, criticism or review, as permitted under the Copyright Act, no part may
be reproduced by any process without the prior permission of the publisher.

A catalogue record for this book is available from the
National Library of New Zealand.

Printed in China by Everbest Printing Co Ltd

Published with the assistance of Ngā Pae o te Māramatanga

CONTENTS

Acknowledgements	vii
Abbreviations	ix

PART ONE: THE CONTEXT

Introduction	3
Privatised Military Industry	9
Conversations within New Zealand about the Privatised Military Industry	23
Reports of Māori in the Industry	33

PART TWO: THE PEOPLE

Land Based Security	41
– T	44
Land Based Logistics	71
– MM	72
Maritime Security	81
– Silver Surfer	82
Owners and Managers	97
– John N	97
– Nigel	111

REFLECTIONS   123

Glossary	141
Bibliography	143
Index	153

ACKNOWLEDGEMENTS

This project began a number of years ago and since that time there have been numerous people and conversations that have helped to shape and refine the ideas in this book.

I would like to first acknowledge and thank the people that I interviewed for the book. They took a chance on a person many of them did not know and shared their stories and personal anecdotes in a generous and open way. That generosity set the tone for my approach in this book – I have sought to uphold the trust of the people that I have interviewed and do justice to retelling their perspectives. To all of those people who met me at noisy cafes, a sports ground, a garden centre, a park bench in a southerly and on skype – thank you.

My second thank you goes to those people who put me in contact with their family members and for helping me to make other contacts – without your support, time and effort there really would not be a book to read.

There were also people who spoke to me 'off the record', to give me a context of issues within New Zealand and overseas and although these narratives are not expressly in the book they certainly provided the details and insights which enabled me to piece the puzzle together.

Thank you to all of those that have worked on the manuscript and made the book possible: Ngā Pae o te Māramatanga for the publication grant; the editorial team and staff at Huia Publishers; to April Henderson and Noelani Goodyear-Ka'opua for insightful feedback on the proposal; and to Tahu Kukutai for translating Statistics New Zealand data into a format I could understand. I am very grateful to Robyn Bargh, Chris Andersen, Bethan Greener, April Henderson and Quentin Whanau for putting aside their numerous work and family commitments to read and provide invaluable suggestions on the manuscript's first draft.

Thank you to Zoe Pearson, David Parr and Bob Young for hosting me while I was conducting interviews and to Ocean Mercier, Brian Tunui, Terese McLeod, Quentin Whanau, Carwyn Jones, Nikki Hessell, Jessica Hutchings, Lydia Wevers, Teresia Teaiwa and Katerina Teaiwa for providing helpful thoughts and advice at various stages. And finally further thanks to other colleagues, friends and family who listened patiently to my chatter about this topic and who, in many cases, unwittingly inspired me.

ABBREVIATIONS

2IC	Second in command
22 SAS	British 22 Special Air Service Regiment
AK	Kalashnikov assault rifle
AK-47	Kalashnikov assault rifle
APC	Armoured personnel carrier
APOD	Aerial Port of Debarkation
BARS	Background Asia Risk Solutions
BIAP	Baghdad International Airport
COO	Chief operating officer
CPP	Cambodian People's Party
CRG	Control Risk Group
CV	Curriculum vitae
DOD	United States Department of Defense
EMSS	Energy and Maritime Security Services LLC
ERG	ERG Partners Financial and Strategic Advisory Firm
GDP	Gross domestic product
ICoC	International Code of Conduct for Private Security Service Providers
IP	Intellectual property

ISPS	International Port and Ship Security Code
IRD	Inland Revenue Department
IZ	International Zone (Baghdad)
KBR	Kellogg Brown and Root
KEA	Kiwi expats abroad
KR	Khmer Rouge
LNs	Local nationals
LOGCAP	Logistics Civilian Augmentation Program
MPRI	Military Professionals Resources Incorporated
MSS	Maritime Security Specialists
NGO	Non-governmental organisation
NPC	National Provincial Championship
NZDF	New Zealand Defence Force
NZRFU	New Zealand Rugby Football Union
NZSAS	New Zealand Special Air Service
PMCs	Private military companies
PMFs	Privatised military firms
PMSCs	Private military and security companies
PSD	Personal security detail
RPGs	Rocket propelled grenades
SARS	Severe acute respiratory syndrome
SF	Special forces
SIS	New Zealand Security Intelligence Service
SNCO	Senior non-commissioned officer, New Zealand Defence Force
SO	Special operations
SOF	Special operations forces

Abbreviations

SOPs	Standard operating procedures
SRU	Singapore Rugby Union
TCNs	Third country nationals
TNCs	Transnational corporations
UN	United Nations
URG	Unity Resources Group
US	United States of America

PART ONE:
THE CONTEXT

INTRODUCTION

In March 2000 New Zealand media reported on the 'secret rescue' of an Indonesian man from somewhere in Indonesia by members of a New Zealand company, Onix International.[1] Comments about the operation by director of the company, Ken Whatuira were reported, as were those of Labour MP at the time John Tamihere, who was alleged to have an interest in the company through his position at the Waipareira Trust, Auckland.[2] What kind of world did Onix and its owners inhabit? And what happened to them and their employees? And what was the connection they appeared to have with the Māori economy?

The year 2000 was a time when internationally private military and security companies (PMSCs) were flourishing but there was little coverage of them in New Zealand. It was a rapidly expanding industry and Ken Whatuira and his colleagues were entering it, as were many other Māori.

Those Māori with a family member in the military would have known in 2000 that the privatised military industry was expanding and that jobs were available. The end of the Cold War and the break-up of a number of states in Europe saw an American company, Military Professionals Resources Incorporated (MPRI), contracted to support in combat operations in Bosnia – eventually changing the course of that civil war.[3] The United Nations (UN) was even beginning to examine, more closely, the role of private companies for peacekeeping and humanitarian missions.[4] The attacks on the New York World Trade Centre in 2001 led to United States invasions in Afghanistan in 2001 and Iraq in 2003. PMSCs were heavily involved in both conflicts and ex-military Māori joined with many others in the lucrative sector.

Why haven't the stories of Māori in this industry been told? There is no straightforward or simple answer to this question. There are factors about the industry itself which may contribute: long-running and often polarised debates about the morality and legality and regulation of companies engaging in military activities which many view as the exclusive domain of states.[5] There is a nature of secrecy in the industry where those working in it do not generally talk about the specifics of each job in case it could jeopardise the safety of themselves or co-workers. It needs to be remembered that most of these jobs take place in or very near war zones where information is a commodity and can lead to attacks on people and assets. In addition, the privatised military industry is closely linked with other industries and entities that are controversial: the arms industry, the oil industry and transnational corporations. These factors combined would surely cause any worker in this industry to pause when discussing their lives, including to journalists or academics.

Perhaps, however, the answers are closer to home. There are particular kinds of perceptions of Māori people and the Māori economy which tend to dominate stories about Māori. Certainly the view that Māori are 'warrior people' is one that might fit in with considering the military industry. But most current research and narratives about Māori are focused on Māori who live in New Zealand and who are involved in reclaiming and reasserting self-determination and fostering the economic development and well-being of their whānau, hapū and iwi. This focus is in part a product of this point in time when Māori land trusts and incorporations are economically stronger and more prominent and hapū and iwi rūnanga are politically and economically stronger and all of these entities are looking for practical research to assist their aims and activities.

Unfortunately, this focus implicitly results in some Māori, particularly those who live or work overseas, being marginalised or excluded from the picture. Some scholars are beginning to explore Māori communities that tend to be marginalised particularly in accounts of the Māori economy. Tahu Kukutai and Paul Hamer, for example, have conducted research on Māori in Australia and the nature of Māori lives and employment in the mining sector.[6] A similar story also needs to be told about Māori in the privatised military industry.

My conservative estimates of Māori within this industry indicate that at least NZ$22 million may be being earned by Māori workers annually. How much of this returns to New Zealand and contributes directly or indirectly to the Māori economy is unknown. The Māori economy is often considered to be based in domestic industries such as agriculture, fisheries and forestry.[7] But what of the hidden economic contributions, both monetary and non-monetary, of Māori contractors from the privatised military industry?

Consider that Māori in this industry are trained originally in the New Zealand military or police force and the New Zealand Army is New Zealand's largest single employer of Māori, with approximately 22 percent of all personnel being Māori.[8] How many of these people go to work for PMSCs? And if we compare the pay, private work clearly has its attractions. In the private sector average annual pay can be around NZ$112,655. A New Zealand Army corporal's annual salary is $55,023 to $63,110.[9]

This book is not an expose. I will not reveal scandalous secrets about people and the companies they work for. The aim of this book is to document the stories of Māori in the privatised military industry and in doing so highlight what I believe to be a hidden aspect of the Māori economy. I will follow the stories of four men and one woman who are, in their own ways, unique and thought-provoking and a central part of this largely undocumented Māori history. I would like this book to encourage people to reflect on who gets included and excluded in current definitions of the Māori economy and whether there are other theoretical frameworks that will help to create better definitions.

After years of researching topics that are connected with neo-liberalism, Māori rights, and my hapū, I came to this topic excited, thinking that it would finally be research that was a step removed from me personally. It should have been obvious, however, from my first interview, someone known to me, and my second interview, someone referred by their sister, and the third, someone referred by their cousin, and the fourth, someone referred by their daughter and so on that this topic was in fact deeply personal. The personal connections have enabled this research to be possible. Without people trusting that I will treat their loved ones with respect and dignity, no one would have spoken with me. And without people telling their stories – tales of food poisoning in Mombasa to playing touch rugby in Basra – this research would have remained a purely theoretical and academic elaboration. And most importantly, it would have missed what I now believe to be crucial – looking at this topic and seeing the people and their whānau connections.

The interviews in this book were conducted in 2013 and 2014. Some were conducted in person; others were conducted via Skype when those interviewed were overseas. There are a number of interviews which did not end up in the book but which provided valuable insights into the context of the industry.

As a result of the secretive nature of this industry, while I have verified as much of the information I received as possible, I also acknowledge that I am letting the stories that people have provided to me stand on their own terms as their versions of events.

The use of pseudonyms was strongly encouraged by the Victoria University of Wellington Human Ethics Committee. This is a contentious industry, about which people hold strong and contrasting views and because the people I have interviewed have families who work in a variety of professions where that might become an issue, interviewees agreed to choose their own pseudonym. Initials have been used throughout interviews when specific individuals are referred to.

The broader ethical and methodological underpinnings of this book are based on kaupapa Māori. Kaupapa Māori research methodologies have become commonplace in the area of Māori studies and aim to support culturally appropriate ways of conducting research with Māori and for that research to be transformative.[10] The purpose of this book is to be supportive of dynamic understandings of the Māori economy. It is premised on valuing relationships between myself, the interviewees and their wider whānau and all interviewees have checked the quotations attributed to them here.

The book is divided into two parts; the first provides an overview of the privatised military industry internationally then turns to consider conversations about the industry that have occurred in New Zealand. I then examine how Māori specifically have been described in relation to the industry, particularly in the media.

Part Two is divided into interviews with T, MM and the Silver Surfer who have worked in the industry in different roles. The interviews with John N.

and Nigel follow: two people who have been in the industry much longer and who have vast experience in management and in John's case also as an owner of a PMSC.

I then conclude with some thoughts about how this book might provide a basis for further research and a broader view of Māori and the Māori economy.

END NOTES

1. Staff reporters, 'Ex-SAS men in secret rescue,' *New Zealand Herald*, 9 March 2000.
2. M. Dearnaley, 'Ex-SAS shocked at condition of hostage tycoon,' *New Zealand Herald*, 10 March 2000.
3. Peter W. Singer, *Corporate Warriors: The Rise of the Privatized Military Industry*, 2nd ed. (Ithaca: Cornell University, 2008), vii.
4. D. Lilly, 'The Privatization of Peacekeeping: Prospects and Realities,' *Disarmament Forum: Peacekeeping Evolution or Extinction?* 3 (Geneva: United Nations, 2000).
5. S. Chesterman and C. Lehnardt, eds., *From Mercenaries to Market: The Rise and Regulation of Private Military Companies* (Oxford: Oxford University Press, 2007); T. Jager and G. Kummel eds., *Private Military Security Companies: Chances, Problems, Pitfalls and Prospects* (Wiesbaden: VS Verlag fur Sozialwissenschaften, 2007).
6. Paul Hamer, *Māori in Australia: Ngā Māori I Te Ao Moemoeā* (Wellington: Te Puni Kōkiri, 2007); T. Kukutai and S. Pawar, 'A Socio-demographic Profile of Māori living in Australia,' NIDEA Working Paper, no. 3 (June 2013).
7. BERL, 'The Māori Economy: A Sleeping Giant?' 22 December 2010.
8. *Te Ara Encyclopedia of New Zealand*, 'Armed Forces', accessed 28 June 2015 http://www.teara.govt.nz/en/graph/35716/defence-force-personnel-by-gender-and-ethnicity-2012. Te Puni Kōkiri put the numbers of Māori in the army at 20% in 2008. (Te Puni Kōkiri, September 2008).
9. 'New Zealand Defence Force website,' accessed 25 January 2015, http://www.defencecareers.mil.nz/army/army-life/salaries-working-conditions.
10. L. Smith, *Decolonising Methodologies* (Otago: Otago University Press, 1999); K. Irwin, 'Māori Research Methods and Practices,' *Sites* 28 (Autumn 1994).

PRIVATISED MILITARY INDUSTRY

In this section, I outline how the privatised military industry has flourished in the past two decades and how we can categorise private military and security companies. There seems to be much agreement that not only is the industry here to stay but is also 'likely to grow, diversify, and become a "mature" industry'.[1] The wars in Iraq and Afghanistan are 'easily the largest privatized conflicts the world has ever seen'.[2] Some have even described them as 'contractor wars'.[3]

Much of the literature around PMSCs points to the very long history of the practice of 'men specialising in warfare'[4] and being paid for it. To distinguish between the older forms of mercenary activity and the nature of the industry today, Peter Singer deliberately uses the term 'privatized military industry'.[5] I also use this term. There continues to be much debate about the distinctions between modern companies and those of the past.

RESONANCES WITH THE PAST

One of the most common refrains in the literature about PMSCs is that their earlier forms were called mercenaries; tales of which date back to the earliest human civilisations where economic and military power became entwined. Daniel Kramer argues that economic and military supremacy are dependent on each other and that this interdependency continues to be integral to the international political economy. Kramer points to the expansion of European states in the sixteenth and seventeenth centuries and how inextricably linked their militaries and their economies were. As one of his examples, Kramer outlines the English East India Company founded in 1599, which was one of the 'forerunners of the modern corporation'.[6] The success of the East India Company and those similar was intimately connected to their ability to use warfare with the sanction of the English Crown – in a sense the Crown had outsourced part of its monopoly on lethal force. In 1661 the East India Company was empowered by the English Crown to 'make war or peace with non-Christian princes or people'.[7] For its economic dominance in India, Kramer explains that the East India Company then relied upon the use of armies which were larger than the British Army and with British officers and 'native troops'.[8]

As Kramer suggests, one of the similarities between historical configurations and the contemporary system is the inextricable connection between creating and maintaining economic power and the use of military force. The second similarity is the use of 'natives' as the predominant bodies used for fighting for that power.

In her book, *Ethnic Soldiers*, Cynthia Enloe documents the way that over the decades many states have used different ethnic groups in the composition of types of forces and in specific ranks. She argues that this hierarchy continues into the privatised military industry. Ultimately she suggests that states will continue to use ethnic hierarchies alongside the increasing 'professionalization, modernization and internationalization of their militaries'.[9]

Other scholars have begun to examine the ways that ethnicity and assumptions about types of peoples are playing a role in the privatised military industry. A number of scholars have begun to explore the ways that the notion of 'martial races' is being utilised in the privatised military industry. Paul Higate has examined the ways that Fijian contractors are constructed as

> members of a martial race, with lines of continuity reaching back to the intervention of the imperial powers who, mirroring the Kamba tribe in Kenya, recruited into the British Army 'believed that certain sections of their subject populations had inherent combative and militaristic qualities that made them naturally suited for military service'.[10]

Amanda Chisholm has conducted research with Gurkhas who expressed pride in their identity as a 'martial race' but complained that this was exploited by PMSCs for an economic gain that was not adequately repaid to Gurkha employees.[11]

Māori have also been portrayed as a martial race.[12] Franchesca Walker has described the way that these assumptions were used initially by the British as part of the New Zealand Wars where

> a dichotomy was formed between the civilized, intelligent warfare pursued by British troops and the 'lower' form of war waged by Māori. One newspaper highlighted this key difference during the wars, distinguishing between the groups' approach to battle: 'A Māori is a fighting animal, while the British soldier is a fighting machine [...] One fought by instinct, the other by rule'.[13]

During subsequent world wars, Walker found the martial race discourse was used by Māori and non-Māori. Māori used it in order to try to add legitimacy to calls for political and economic equality and in 1942 Apirana Ngata famously described Māori participation as warriors in the Second World War as 'the price of citizenship' to the new Pākehā settler state. The discourse of Māori as a martial race endures and is now reinforced by the New Zealand Army which in 1994 adopted the name of 'Ngāti Tūmatauenga' (the tribe of the God of War).

THE RISE OF THE PRIVATISED MILITARY INDUSTRY

The expansion of the privatised military industry is often seen as the culmination of two key factors – the end of the Cold War and the influence of neo-liberal policies. The first of these is relatively simple to explain. The end of the Cold War in the early 1990s brought a downscaling of militaries in many countries and a flood of personnel looking for work. It was also followed by civil wars including in the regions of the former Yugoslavia where state boundaries were being redrawn and contested.[14] As a result of the politically sensitive nature domestically in the United States of their involvement in these civil wars, private companies were seen as a way to be involved but at an arm's length.[15]

The second issue: that of the dominance of neo-liberal policies since the 1980s having supported the flourishing of the privatised military industry is somewhat more complex.[16] Core neo-liberal assumptions about the superiority of 'the market' to deliver services to communities has led governments in the

United States, Britain, New Zealand and many other countries in the world to reduce the size of the state by corporatising state-owned enterprises or privatising them. Neo-liberal adherents argue that the market is the best mechanism to provide for the desires of self-maximising buyers and sellers and military functions are simply another set of services that can be best provided by private companies.[17]

Andrew Bearpark and Sabrina Schulz argue that by contracting out military functions states, themselves, have created the market where PMSCs have work.[18] They suggest that states benefit from the privatisation of security services because the private sector assists in transforming the armed forces particularly by investing in high-tech military hardware; the private sector provides jobs for personnel leaving the British Army which means 'the job gets done despite the downsizing of the armed forces'.[19] This line of argument resonates with neo-liberal advocates who suggest that the private sector, through their profit-seeking motives is better placed to develop military products and military services than a state and that as state militaries downsize many of them no longer have a force which can be deployed at the speed of PMSCs.[20]

There is a strong connection between neo-liberal policies and the success of large transnational corporations.[21] Transnational corporations are commonly vertically integrated and are able to capitalise on the fluctuation of commodity prices or labour costs by moving across the globe where these factors of production are cheapest. Neo-liberal policies have a tendency to support transnational corporations as their private sector advice on business is seen as valuable in the management of corporatised state assets and this, in turn, often provides them a greater voice in policy formulation.[22]

In addition to this, transnational corporations are commonly those contracted to provide military and security services and are many of the largest and wealthiest of those contracted. This situation makes it harder for smaller companies to compete and many end up being bought out by the larger companies or entering subcontracting arrangements.[23] Singer argues that although it is possible for smaller companies, like those in New Zealand or from less-developed countries, to get some work, on the whole the 'market seems to have a tendency toward consolidation and the larger international firms will be able to make quite attractive offers at the outset to induce the best smaller firms to link up'.[24]

PRIVATE MILITARY AND SECURITY COMPANIES: IDENTIFYING AS A BUSINESS

Whether they are transnational or smaller in scale, many PMSCs have specific corporate identities. Singer's most well-known definition of private military and security companies provides a starting point to begin thinking about the form that these companies take. Singer argues that what he calls 'privatized military firms' (PMFs) are

> business organizations that trade in professional services intricately linked to warfare. They are corporate bodies that specialize in the provision of military skills, including combat operations, strategic planning, intelligence, risk assessment, operational support, training, and technical skills ... PMFs are private business entities that deliver to consumers a wide spectrum of military and security services, once generally assumed to be exclusively inside the public context.[25]

Singer argues that privatised military firms can be distinguished from what people describe as 'mercenaries' in three key ways. Firstly, PMFs are organised in a business form. They are

> commercial enterprises first and foremost. They are hierarchically organized into registered businesses that trade and compete openly (for the most part) and are vertically integrated into the wide global marketplace. They target market niches by offering packaged services covering a wide variety of military skill sets.[26]

Secondly he argues they are driven by 'business profit rather than individual profit. PMFs function as registered trade units, not as personal black-market ventures for individual profit or adventure.'[27] Finally Singer argues they compete on the open market. 'PMFs are considered legal entities bound to their employers by recognized contracts and in many cases at least nominally their home states by law requiring registration, periodic reporting, and licensing of foreign contracts.'[28]

As former commanding officer for the New Zealand Special Air Service (NZSAS), Jim Blackwell argues it is this image of a professional, corporate and responsible *business* that PMSCs treasure.

> ... unlike mercenaries who deny their existence, most PMCs [private military companies] publicly advertise their services, including maintaining their own websites. Many are publicly listed companies and so must comply with the reporting and disclosure requirements associated with that status. This demonstrates a desire for good public relations and a positive image.[29]

Benedict Sheehy et al. also argue that what they term 'private military corporations' have a predominantly business identity.

> ... from a legal perspective, the PMC is not different from any other business corporations in that it has the same structure, rights, duties, and obligations. It is controlled by a board of directors, has shareholders who hope to receive dividends from corporate profit, and engages in activity with the sole purpose of turning a profit.[30]

The unique status of PMSCs as corporations that can engage in lethal force has dangers, however, according to Sheehy et al. as this identity enables the corporation's 'human actors [to] act with impunity to a degree not enjoyed in any other arena of human activity'.[31] As an example of what they describe as impunity, they point out that whereas many other companies would be liable for deaths caused by their company, and indeed even the United States military has paid compensation to families of civilians killed by their military, PMSCs are often not held responsible for deaths caused by their personnel.[32]

As PMSCs are businesses which aim to make a profit, like many large corporations they are interested in creative ways to ensure they maximise profits. Some scholars have suggested PMSCs may be willing to prolong conflicts so that they continue to have work; however, this idea would seem to contradict the image that PMSCs rely on, of being able to efficiently and swiftly complete their contracts.[33]

Others scholars, such as Andrew Feinstein, have suggested PMSCs have managed to sustain profits by ensuring their companies are vertically integrated. Vertical integration enables companies to perform a range of services that link together. For example, they may be registered in a country where tax rates are low but build a piece of equipment in another country and repair it somewhere else where labour costs are even lower. Feinstein points to Lockheed Martin as an exemplar of this practice that has services for every aspect of war, 'from targeting to intervention, and from occupation to interrogation'.[34]

Feinstein provides an additional example of a practice that he argues allows significant profits for particular companies that have vertical integration or diverse portfolios. He argues the practice of 'reset' which is a 'policy whereby the US military continually repairs, upgrades or simply replaces military equipment that has been used on the field of combat. This "resets" the equipment and units that use them to their operational level as it existed prior to the conflicts'.[35] PMSCs are those companies which are contracted to do this work and or which sell the US military the new equipment. Considering the quantities of equipment involved – the United States Army alone had US$30 billion worth of equipment stationed in Iraq and Afghanistan by early 2007[36], to 'reset' and replace this equipment has provided a lucrative income for a few PMSCs.

The sums of money involved in the privatised military industry loom in the billions of dollars making it a potentially lucrative business opportunity. Feinstein places the total US Department of Defense War Budget Authority for 2004 to 2011 at US$1,105 billion.[37] Of that he suggests US$141.9 billion was spent on military personnel. A study for the United States Congress determined that 'Over the last six fiscal years, DOD [US Department of Defense] obligations for contracts performed in the Iraq and Afghanistan areas of operation were approximately $160 billion and exceeded total contract obligations of any other U.S. federal agency'.[38]

One of the best ways to illustrate the size and speed of the expansion of the privatised military industry is to compare the Gulf War of 1991 and the Iraq war after the 2003 US-led invasion. In the Gulf War of 1991 the ratio of US troops to private contractors was about sixty-to-one.[39] In Iraq in 2007, private contractors outnumbered US troops. While the official US military presence was 160,000 troops that year, if the approximately 180,000 private contractors of varying nationalities were added, all of whom were working for the US objectives, it gives a better sense of just how the military sector and power dynamics have changed.[40]

INTERNATIONAL REGULATION

One of the other dynamics that have changed in the international arena is an increasing focus on regulation of PMSCs. There are a number of international conventions and documents that aim to regulate PMSCs internationally. The first is the United Nations (UN) International Convention against the Recruitment, Use, Financing and Training of Mercenaries (Mercenary Convention). Discussions about mercenary activities at the United Nations go back to the 1960s and the General Assembly's adoption of the Declaration on the Granting of Independence to Colonial Countries and Peoples which included a number of resolutions on mercenaries.[41] Over the years these resolutions were amended and in 1977 Nigeria, in co-operation with other African states, proposed the idea of an international convention. The International Convention against the Recruitment, Use, Financing and Training of Mercenaries was drafted and discussed in working groups until eventually being adopted by the General Assembly and opened for signatories and ratification in 1989. It came into force in 2001.

While the UN Mercenary Convention uses the controversial term 'mercenaries', in 2008 its mandate was extended to encompass the activities of PMSCs,

> including to study the effects of PMSC activities on the enjoyment of human rights and to draft basic international principles that encourage respect for human rights by these companies. The expansion of our mandate reflects the depth of the Human Rights Council's concerns about the proliferation of PMSCs. Indeed, in the last decade, many States, international organizations, NGOs and transnational corporations have become increasingly dependent on PMSCs to provide services that have historically been within the domain of States.[42]

A UN working group monitors the Mercenary Convention. In 2010 the United Nations General Assembly passed a resolution to create an open-ended intergovernmental working group to 'consider the possibility of elaborating an international regulatory framework on the regulation, monitoring and oversight of the activities of private military and security companies'.[43] The open-ended working group has now drafted a 'possible' convention specifically relating to PMSCs.[44]

Operating parallel to the UN instruments is the International Code of Conduct for Private Security Service Providers (ICoC) 2010 which is a 'Swiss Government convened, multi-stakeholder initiative that aims to both clarify international standards for the private security industry operating in complex environments, as well as to improve oversight and accountability of these companies'.[45]

New Zealand companies that were signatories to the ICoC in 2014 include:

- AKTS NZ LTD, signed by: Karl Plas, director, headquarters: New Zealand, Waikato, Cambridge, website: www.aktsnz.com[46]
- Barantas Security Group, signed by: Gary Crook, managing director, headquarters: New Zealand, Auckland, website: www.barantas.co.nz
- Hardcastle Security, signed by: Steven Hardcastle, director, headquarters: New Zealand, Palmerston North, website: www.hardcastlesecurity.com
- NavSec International Limited, signed by: Brian Sloan, managing director, headquarters: New Zealand, Auckland, website: www.navsec.co.nz
- Valour Security, signed by: William Brown, CEO, headquarters: New Zealand, Auckland, website: www.valoursecurity.com

Other signatories that have indicated links to New Zealand but which may not have their headquarters in New Zealand include:

- Energy and Maritime Security Services, LLC (EMSS), signed by: Alan Brosnan, president, headquarters: United States, Mississippi, Horn Lake, website: www.emssllc.com
- Envoy360, signed by Samuel Stevenson, CEO, headquarters: United Arab Emirates, Dubai, website: www.envoy360.com

- Near East Security Services, signed by: Richard Terzan, CEO, headquarters Iraq, Baghdad, website: www.neareastsecurity.com
- Thai Maritime Solutions Co. Ltd, signed by: Stephen Poka, director of operations, headquarters: Thailand, Bangkok, website: www.thaimaritimesolutions.com
- Trojan Global Protection 254, signed by: Justin Brinkies, managing director, headquarters: Australia, Adelaide, website: www.trojanglobalprotection.com.au

The ICoC is voluntary but the desire of companies to publicly sign up to it suggests that companies see it as important to distinguish themselves from 'rogue' operators, who tend to avoid scrutiny in order to conduct illegal military operations.

Another Swiss initiative is the Montreux Document on Pertinent International Legal Obligations and Good Practices for States related to Operations of Private Military and Security Companies during Armed Conflict, 2008 which has received widespread ratification by states including the New Zealand Government in 2013.[47] The Montreux Document defines 'how international law applies to the activities of private military and security companies when they are operating in an armed conflict zone. It contains a set of good practices designed to help states take measures nationally in order to fulfil their obligations under international law'.[48]

Discussions around the international regulation of PMSCs highlight the different actors that use the services of PMSCs such as international organisations, NGOs (non-governmental organisations) global corporations and wealthy individuals.[49] Although there is a great deal of overlap between the activities of these different actors, generally the three main contractors of privatised military work include: governments, transnational corporations and NGOs. Governments seek out PMSCs to support either their own regimes or the protection of their own interests and resources. The most well known is the United States Department of Defense contracting companies to assist with the wars in Iraq and Afghanistan[50], but other examples include Somalia where PMSCs were employed in the 1990s to assist local Somali people to patrol their maritime areas and protect their fisheries stocks against illegal fishers.[51]

Transnational corporations, particularly those in resource extractive areas like oil, gas, and gold commonly use PMSCs both onshore and offshore in areas of the world where their extractive activities are either hotly opposed or exist within states at war.[52] Singer suggests that in conflict zones PMSCs act as '"investment enablers" providing clients with robust security that make otherwise extremely risky investment options safe enough to be financially viable'.[53] In countries like Algeria, Singer suggests that oil firms spend 'close to 9 per cent of their operational budget on military-style protection'.[54]

International organisations, such as those of the United Nations and non-governmental organisations also contract the services of PMSCs often when trying to conduct their humanitarian work in countries that are at war. Activities such as demining or delivering humanitarian aid now rely on contracts with PMSCs. Whereas PMSCs assist transnational corporations as 'investment enablers' Singer argues they in turn assist NGOs as 'aid enablers'.[55] Being hired to assist with humanitarian work provides significant credibility to those PMSCs involved as they are then perceived as more ethical and reputable.[56]

There is much debate about whether governments should be engaging PMSCs to in effect be their 'state agents'[57] when there are such limited controls and regulation over the actions of PMSCs. Indeed much of the literature about PMSCs revolves around how states can better regulate PMSCs. Gabor Rona, an expert on the working group on the use of mercenaries, argues that PMSCs are corporations with corporate responsibilities and should ensure they respect human rights and do not infringe the human rights of others.[58] In the next section I explore how some of these conversations about regulation at the international level have been articulated in New Zealand.

END NOTES

1. A. Bearpark and S. Schulz, 'The Future of the Market,' in *From Mercenaries to Market*, eds. Chesterman and Lehnardt,, 243.
2. A. Feinstein, *The Shadow World: Inside the Global Arms Trade* (London: Penguin, 2012), 403.
3. Ibid.

4 D. Kramer, 'Does History Repeat Itself? A Comparative Analysis of Private Military Entities,' in *Private Military Security Companies*, eds. Jager and Kummel, 23.

5 Singer, *Corporate Warriors*, 2008.

6 Kramer, 'Does History Repeat Itself?', 25.

7 Ibid.

8 Ibid.

9 C.H. Enloe, *Ethnic Soldiers: State Security in a Divided Society* (Middlesex: Penguin, 1980), 234.

10 P. Higate, 'Martial Races and Enforcement Masculinities of the Global South: Weaponising Fijian, Chilean and Salvadoran Postcoloniality in the Mercenary Sector,' *Globalizations* 9, no. 1 (2012): 43.

11 A. Chisholm, 'The Silenced and Indispensible,' *International Feminist Journal of Politics* (2013).

12 M.F. Erai, 'Māori Soldiers: Māori Experiences of the New Zealand Army' (master's thesis, Victoria University of Wellington, 1995).

13 F. Walker, 'Descendants of a Warrior Race: the Māori Contingent, the Pioneer Battalion and the Martial Race Myth 1914-1919,' *War and Society* 31, no.1 (2012): 7-8.

14 Singer, *Corporate Warriors*, 2008, 4.

15 Ibid.

16 W. Bello, *Deglobalization: Ideas for a New World Economy* (London: Zed Books, 2004).

17 D. Bandow, 'Privatizing Military Maintenance,' *CATO Institute*; see also C. Bourge, 'Analysis: Mercenary as Future Peacekeeper?' United Press International news, August 2003.

18 Bearpark and Schulz, 'The Future of the Market,' 242.

19 Ibid

20 D. Brooks and M. Chorev, 'Ruthless humanitarianism: Why Marginalizing Private Peacekeeping Kills People,' in *Private military and security companies: Ethics, Policies and Civil-Military Relations*, eds. A. Alexandra, D. Baker and M. Caparini (London: Routledge, 2008).

21 S. George, *The Lugano Report: On Preserving Capitalism in the Twenty-First Century* (London: Pluto Press, 1999).

22 S. George, *Whose Crisis, Whose Future?* (London: Polity Press, 2013).

23 D. Avant, *The Market for Force* (Cambridge: Cambridge University Press, 2006), 180.

24 Singer, *Corporate Warriors*, 2008, 87.

25 Ibid, 8.

26 Ibid, 45.

27 Ibid, 46.

28 Ibid.

29 J.W. Blackwell, 'Private Military Companies: Their Emergence, Role and Impact on NZ Army Special Operations Personnel Turnover', (unpublished dissertation, University of Leicester, 2006), 13.

30 B. Sheehy, J. Maogoto and V. Newell, *Legal Control of the Private Military Corporation* (Hampshire,: Palgrave Macmillan, 2009), 35.

31 Ibid, 45.

32 Ibid, 48.

33 R.D. Wallwork, 'Operational Implications of Private Military Companies in the Global War on Terror,' School of Advanced Military Studies, United States Army Command and General Staff College, (Fort Leavenworth, Kansas, 2005).

34 Feinstein, *The Shadow World*, 413.

35 Ibid, 410.

36 Ibid.

37 Ibid, 412.

38 M. Schwartz and J. Church, 'Department of Defense's Use of Contractors to Support Military Operations: Background Analysis and Issues for Congress,' Congressional Research Service (Washington, 2013), 2.

39 J. Scahill, 'War on Iraq' (13 August 2007).

40 Ibid.

41 United Nations, 'Procedural History of the International Convention against the Recruitment, Use, Financing and Training of Mercenaries General Assembly resolution 44/34' (New York, 4 December 1989), accessed 25 June 2014, http://legal.un.org/avl/ha/icruftm/icruftm.html

42 Gabor Rona, 'Remarks,' (presented to UN Working Group on the Use of Mercenaries, Montreux +5 Conference, 11–13 December 2013).

43 'Office of the Commissioner for Human Rights, United Nations Human Rights Council,' http://www.ohchr.org/EN/HRBodies/HRC/WGMilitary/Pages/OEIWGMilitaryIndex.aspx

44 'Human Rights Council, 2011, A/HRC/WG.10/1/2,' accessed 6 January 2015, http://psm.du.edu/media/documents/international_regulation/united_nations/human_rights_council_and_ga/open_ended_wg/session_1/un_open_ended_wg_session_1_draft-of-a-possible-convention.pdf

45 'ICoC website,' accessed 24 March 2014, http://www.icoc-psp.org/About_ICoC.html

46 'ICoC Signatory Companies List,' accessed 24 March 2014, http://www.icoc-psp.org/uploads/Signatory_Companies_-_August_2013_-_Composite_List2.pdf

47 'Swiss Federal Department of Foreign Affairs website,' accessed 22 December 2014, https://www.eda.admin.ch/eda/en/fdfa/foreign-policy/international-law/international-humanitarian-law/private-military-security-companies/participating-states.html

48 Swiss Federal Department of Foreign Affairs, 'The Montreux Document', accessed 22 December 2014, https://www.eda.admin.ch/eda/en/fdfa/foreign-policy/international-law/international-humanitarian-law/private-military-security-companies/montreux-document.html

49 Avant, *The Market for Force*, 7.

50 Ibid, 8.

51 Jatin Dua, 'A Pirate's Life for Me,' *New Internationalist*, September 2013, 15–17.

52 Singer, *Corporate Warriors*, 2008, 80–81.

53 Ibid, 81.

54 Ibid.

55 Ibid, 82.

56 Ibid, 83.

57 J. Cockayne, 'Make or Buy? Principal-agent theory and the regulation of private military companies,' in *From Mercenaries to Market*, eds. Chesterman and Lehnardt, 196.

58 Rona, 'Remarks.'

CONVERSATIONS WITHIN NEW ZEALAND ABOUT THE PRIVATISED MILITARY INDUSTRY

By the end of 2001 when the UN Mercenary Convention came into effect, the privatised military industry was expanding and questions about how it was to be best regulated were prevalent in many countries. In New Zealand the questions about regulation made a clear reference back to the 1997 case of the Papua New Guinean Government contracting a PMSC. The 'Sandline Affair' as it became colloquially known, came to a tense conclusion when it was revealed by the media that the Papua New Guinean Government had contracted Sandline, owned by former British Army officer Tim Spicer, to conduct military activities in Bougainville. Spicer and Sandline personnel were subsequently expelled from Papua New Guinea. When Phil Goff introduced the Mercenary Activities (Prohibition) Bill into the New Zealand Parliament in 2003, he cited the Sandline case as an impetus for the New Zealand Government to indicate that 'the use of mercenaries is unacceptable as a method of conflict resolution'.[1] The debates about this bill and subsequent act provide a rich history of the discussion about regulation in New Zealand.

In March 2002 the New Zealand Government had conducted a review of its participation in United Nations treaties and decided to respond to the UN Secretary General's call for states to become parties to more UN conventions to ensure their effectiveness.[2] During the first reading of the Mercenary Activities (Prohibition) Bill in the New Zealand Parliament, Phil Goff made it clear that the Mercenary Activities (Prohibition) Bill was simply the legislation needed to enable the New Zealand Government to become party to the international

Mercenary Convention. He argued that the New Zealand Government 'has long opposed the use of mercenaries'[3] and that 'These new offences will discourage the use of New Zealand as a base for mercenary activities'.[4]

The bill was eventually passed under urgency in June 2004. The final act defines a mercenary as:

- (1)In this Act, unless the context otherwise requires, **mercenary** means—
    - (a) any person—
        - (i) who is recruited, within New Zealand or elsewhere, in order to take part in hostilities in an armed conflict; and
        - (ii) whose purpose, or one of whose purposes, in taking part in hostilities in the armed conflict is making private gain; and
        - (iii) who is promised or paid by, or on behalf of, a party to the armed conflict material compensation substantially in excess of that promised or paid to combatants of similar rank and functions in the armed forces of that party; or
    - (b) any person, other than a person referred to in paragraph (a),—
        - (i) who is recruited, within New Zealand or elsewhere, in order to take part in a concerted act of violence; and
        - (ii) whose purpose, or one of whose purposes, in taking part in the concerted act of violence is making significant private gain; and
        - (iii) who is promised or paid material compensation.
- (2) A person is not a mercenary—
    - (a) within the meaning of subsection (1)(a) if he or she is—
        - (i) a citizen of a party to the armed conflict or ordinarily resident in territory controlled by a party to the armed conflict; or
        - (ii) a member of the armed forces of a party to the armed conflict; or
        - (iii) sent by a State that is not a party to the armed conflict on official duty as a member of its armed forces:

- (b) within the meaning of subsection (1) (b) if he or she is—
  - (i) a citizen of, or ordinarily resident in, the State against which the concerted act of violence is directed; or
  - (ii) sent by a State on official duty; or
  - (iii) a member of the armed forces of the State on whose territory the concerted act of violence is undertaken.
- (3) A person is not a mercenary within the meaning of subsection (1) (a) or subsection (1) (b) if he or she is taking part in—
  - (a) a peace support mission—
    - (i) for any of the purposes of the United Nations; or
    - (ii) that is undertaken in accordance with the principles of the Charter of the United Nations; or
  - (b) the detection, clearance, deactivation, or destruction of mines or unexploded ordnance, other than in a combat role; or
  - (c) the delivery of humanitarian aid; or
  - (d) domestic policing duties or other lawful activities of a similar kind involving the protection of individuals or property.
- (4) Subsections (2) and (3) do not limit the circumstances in which a person is not a mercenary.[5]

During the select committee process and debates in parliament the main criticisms of the bill revolved around the definition of a 'mercenary'. Ron Mark from New Zealand First was particularly vocal about the bill and argued the definition would include too many people such as former New Zealander soldiers working for PMSCs. He pointed out that he, as a former soldier, had worked for the Sultan of Oman in charge of special forces and queried whether he could be included in the mercenary definition.[6] Other Members of Parliament such as Judith Collins and Stephen Franks also questioned whether former New Zealand Defence Force (NZDF) personnel working in Iraq would be captured by the act. Collins argued that such private military work was a logical career path for soldiers given their training and they should not be inhibited from pursuing a career after the defence force.[7]

In its report on submissions, the Ministry of Foreign Affairs and Trade argued that the ambit of the act would not be so wide:

> The Mercenaries [sic] Convention was never intended to cover all mercenaries but rather is directed at a small group of so-called 'true' or traditional mercenaries: unaffiliated individuals ('freelancers') who are prepared to fight wars or overthrow governments or commit certain terrorist acts for money.[8]

The report went on to acknowledge that the New Zealand Government, in deciding to become party to the Mercenary Convention was aware of arguments for a broader definition but at this stage wanted in the main to 'draw a line around the particular group to be caught ... those mercenaries at the so-called "sharp-end" who engage in hostilities during a war (i.e. in combat) for money'.[9]

Sheehy et al. have criticised the Mercenary Activities (Prohibition) Act and argue that it is not a model that should be promoted for dealing with modern-day private military corporation. At best this type of legislation draws a line in the sand and indicates that a state will not tolerate the traditional, individual dog of war. The issue of whether or not private military corporations should be regulated, and if so, to what end, is a debate that New Zealand is yet to have.[10]

One of the biggest issues with the definition of a mercenary in the act is the lack of clarity about whom it is intended to capture. People might be contracted in a security role and clearly be involved in the daily use of a weapon, returning fire during daily activities (say in Baghdad), but may not necessarily have these activities spelled out *in their contract*. Are they 'mercenaries' or private military and security contractors? In addition, as Ron Mark pointed out in parliamentary debates, it is also intended to capture recruiters but if recruiters come to New Zealand they will not admit to recruiting people to 'take part in hostilities in an armed conflict', but rather will argue they are here to 'recruit people to go and do some security work'.[11] The purpose of the act with its current definition remains unclear.

Green Party Member of Parliament Keith Locke argued in the debates that the New Zealand Defence Force was complicit in enabling recruitments for PMSCs from its own ranks. Sue Kedgley (on behalf of Keith Locke) argued that

> There certainly may be New Zealand mercenaries in Iraq. We know that six former members of the police's Special Tactics Group have gone there, as have former SAS people, and they should know that when they do, they may have trouble with this law if they use arms in military hostilities in Iraq. Their Kiwi recruiters need to be aware of that too. Companies like Red Key Security are advertising in New Zealand papers.
>
> The Green Party is disturbed about the complicity of the New Zealand Defence Force in that recruitment. For example, Brigadier Southwell provided a testimonial for a Defence Force sergeant who resigned last year to operate in Iraq. The brigadier wrote that he had no hesitation in recommending the sergeant as a leader of a close protection team in even the most severe of security situations. If this Bill had been passed at that time, Brigadier Southwell could arguably have been caught up in its provisions and ended up before the courts, if that close protection team had been proved to be a mercenary unit.[12]

It is doubtful the NZDF would have seen things that way. By the early 2000s former commanding officers and soldiers were secretly contacting friends who they thought might be interested in private work, but from a management and organisational level the NZDF was very concerned about retaining staff and opposed active external recruiting. Peter Singer notes that trying to retain personnel was a huge issue for special forces like the SAS.

> This issue has become especially pointed for Special Forces units, which have the most skills and are thus the most marketable. Elite force commanders in Australia, New Zealand, the United Kingdom, and the United States have all expressed deep concern over the poaching of their numbers by PMFs.[13]

In his research Blackwell has noted that special operations command personnel have been unhappy about their soldiers being poached by private companies and in some cases tried to establish a compromise whereby they 'would verify the credibility and competence of their *ex-unit* members in exchange for the PMCs not actively enticing serving soldiers to leave'.[14]

In the report on submissions, the Ministry of Foreign Affairs and Trade voiced some scepticism about the likelihood of prosecutions under the Mercenaries Act but argued that prosecution was not the main aim of the act. 'Even if there are few prosecutions the existence of these crimes will act as a deterrent to those New Zealanders who might contemplate becoming a mercenary and also will ensure that mercenaries from other countries do not regard New Zealand as a safe haven'.[15]

As of 2014, the attorney-general had received no requests for prosecutions under the Mercenary Activities (Prohibition) Act which suggests that it is possible the act has acted as a deterrent as the Ministry of Foreign Affairs and Trade hoped or more likely that the new offences it created have not been actively pursued and the act has had little impact at all.

Many of the conversations about PMSCs in New Zealand have been conducted by those in the NZDF attempting to retain their personnel from the lure of higher salaries in privatised military work. And indeed, the issue of pay and personnel retention in the NZDF has been an ongoing issue. Since 2000, the NZDF has used a number of tactics to try to retain personnel. Pay increases in 2001, 2002 and 2003 began to temporarily bring some of the attrition rates down but pay parity between NZDF personnel and market rates and conditions continues to be difficult.[16] In his 2003 presentation on future challenges to SOF in the fight against global terrorism, an SAS squadron commander noted that 'innovative recruiting techniques, pay scale reviews and adjustment in conditions of service will become necessary components to consider when attracting suitable candidates'.[17] Blackwell argues that in 2003, 2004 and 2005 the numbers of personnel leaving the New Zealand Army 'rocketed'. While the rate for 2000-02 was 10 percent, in '2003 they rocketed to 17 per cent, 2004 28 per cent and 2005 15 per cent'.[18]

The issue of pay rates and NZDF attrition are closely linked. One of the major difficulties for the military is that personnel cannot be easily recruited for the NZDF from other industries as they need to be trained with a specific combination of skills before they are 'ready for work'. As with other professions, like the medical profession, the New Zealand taxpayer was in effect supporting the training of personnel who were then leaving for the private sector where they could attract higher wages.[19] For many years the NZDF has been concerned about its inability to recruit and then retain enough personnel to keep its forces fully functioning, a fact noted in nearly all the annual reports since 2000. In 2003 the NZDF was in a particularly difficult position with the territorial force for example at '50% of its established strength'.[20] In the 2000s the NZDF contracted market research in order to better promote the military as a career and lifestyle and for 2002-03 adopted 'aggressive recruitment strategies'.[21]

Blackwell's research specifically about those who have left the special operations (SO) for private work, involved interviews and responses from questionnaires from people who had left the New Zealand Army in the years 2000 to 2005. Blackwell's findings indicate that although not all personnel left to join PMSCs, those who did leave to pursue private military work did so primarily for the money. 'Without exception, the twenty four survey respondents who left the NZ Army SO unit in the past five years with the intention of becoming a private military contractor did so for the money'.[22] He found that 'private military contracting is considered to be a short term opportunity to establish long term financial security'.[23]

One of the difficulties with this situation, as Blackwell points out, is that the original military ethos for special forces units is to serve the nation selflessly. The privatised military industry interferes with this ethos when specifically targeting special forces personnel who are then motivated by financial gain.

In 2006 the issue of pay was raised in the New Zealand media with claims that SAS soldiers were paid only $4.57 per hour while working in Afghanistan.[24] A statement attributed in the article to NZDF staff indicated that 'The New Zealand Defence Force does not benchmark against private security contractors and is unable to match the wages these organisations can offer'.[25] In 2007 then prime minister Helen Clark suggested the issue of retaining staff was difficult because of low unemployment in New Zealand, presumably meaning people had options other than the military.[26]

The other related issue for the NZDF was whether to let people back into the military once they had taken leave or left the NZDF for overseas private work. Changes were made to the defence force orders following the Mercenary Activities (Prohibition) Act that clearly set out the new requirements. If personnel wanted to take leave without pay to work overseas in paramilitary-type work, they were able to make a request to do so, but only for work that was of a 'logistic or support' nature – not of a 'security or law enforcement nature'.[27] In addition, any references written for personnel would be limited to including only a 'personal testimonial detailing the member of the NZDF character and suitability for civilian employment' and could not 'identify the referee as a member of the NZDF, and NZDF or Service letterhead is not to be used'.[28]

There were concerns for the NZDF about how to adequately security check personnel coming back into the force after being in places like the Middle East. In those kinds of locations personnel may have come into contact with people with views contrary to those of the NZDF and it may not be clear whether they are working for those parties. The chance of security breaches was seen to be slim and the ongoing pressure to maintain personnel numbers soon forced the NZDF to relax the rules and let people back in. Blackwell notes, for example, that from 2005 to 2006 three former soldiers who had previously left the special operations unit were reengaged.[29]

The NZDF was not the only part of the New Zealand Government concerned about what New Zealanders were doing overseas in the privatised military industry. The Inland Revenue Department (IRD) also began to take a close look at the tax implications for this increasingly large group of workers. Although IRD claims it never specifically targeted the workers in the privatised military sector, apparently coincidentally many contractors found themselves facing IRD audits. Although IRD denies any collusion, anecdotal evidence suggests there must have been information sharing between the Department of Customs, Immigration and IRD to identify people working in well-known privatised military industry locations like Iraq.

Africa and the Middle East
Courtesy of the University of Texas Libraries, The University of Texas at Austin
http://www.lib.utexas.edu/maps/africa/africa_pol_2012.pdf

Middle East
Courtesy of the University of Texas Libraries, The University of Texas at Austin
http://www.lib.utexas.edu/maps/middle_east_and_asia/middle_east_pol_2012.pdf

23 Ibid, 57.
24 D. Fisher, 'SAS Soldiers on $4.57 an Hour to Hunt Osama,' *New Zealand Herald*, Sunday 30 April, 2006.
25 Ibid.
26 Helen Clark, 'NZDF No. 48 Command Staff Course' (Speech, 11 December 2007).
27 NZDF, 'Part 9, Chapter 10: Paramilitary Employment,' in *Defence Force Order 3: Human Resources Manual,* 2010), 10.
28 Ibid, 11.
29 Blackwell, Private Military Companies,' 57.

END NOTES

1. Phil Goff, 'Mercenary Activities (Prohibition) Bill: First Reading' (*Hansard*, 5 November 2003).
2. Ministry of Foreign Affairs and Trade, 'Mercenary Activities (Prohibition) Bill: Report on Submissions,' (15 March 2004), 5.
3. Goff, 'Mercenary Activities (Prohibition) Bill: First Reading.'
4. Ibid.
5. 'Mercenary Activities (Prohibtion) Act 2004,' accessed 25 June 2014, http://www.legislation.govt.nz/act/public/2004/0069/latest/DLM304840.html.
6. Ron Mark, 'Mercenary Activities (Prohibition) Bill:, First Reading.'
7. Judith Collins, 'Mercenary Activities (Prohibition) Bill: Second Reading' (*Hansard*, 29 June 2004).
8. Ministry of Foreign Affairs and Trade, Report on Submissions, 2.
9. Ibid.
10. Sheehy, Maogoto, and Newell, *Legal Control of the Private Military Corporation*, 130.
11. Mark, 'Mercenary Activities (Prohibition) Bill: Second Reading' (*Hansard*, 29 June 2004).
12. Sue Kedgley, 'Mercenary Activities (Prohibition) Bill: Second Reading'.
13. Peter Singer, 'Outsourcing War,' *Foreign Affairs* 84, no. 2 (2005): 119–132.
14. Blackwell, 'Private Military Companies,' 46. (emphasis added)
15. Ministry of Foreign Affairs and Trade, 'Report on Submissions,' (15 March 2004) 5.
16. Finance and Expenditure Select Committee 'Standard Estimates Questionnaire 2002/2003, Vote: Defence Force,' (Financial Report, 2002/2003), 9–10.
17. Anonymous Squadron Commander, 'Future Challenges to SOF in the Fight Against Global Terrorism (Brief to PASOC, February 2003), 6.
18. Blackwell, 'Private Military Companies,' 31.
19. 'Junior doctors' pay increase won't keep them here,' *Southland Times*, 10 October 2008.
20. NZDF, 'NZDF Response to Foreign Affairs, Defence and Trade Select Committee' (Questionnaire, 16 October 2003), 17.
21. NZDF, 'Annual Report For the Year Ended 30 June 2003' (Report, 2003), 9.
22. Blackwell, 'Private Military Companies,' 41.

Southeast Asia
Courtesy of the University of Texas Libraries, The University of Texas at Austin
http://www.lib.utexas.edu/maps/middle_east_and_asia/southeast_asia_ref_2012.pdf#page=1&zoom=auto,-12,520

Political Map of the World, August 2013

World Map (Political)
Courtesy of the University of Texas Libraries, The University of Texas at Austin
http://www.lib.utexas.edu/maps/world_maps/world_pol_2013.pdf

REPORTS OF MĀORI IN THE INDUSTRY

A number of media reports about Māori in the privatised military industry over the years have provided some insights into how the industry and Māori involvement might be perceived in New Zealand.

When *The New Zealand Herald* broke the story about personnel from Onix International Ltd rescuing an Indonesian national from Indonesia and bringing him to New Zealand, the company had already been operating for two years. Onix International Ltd was incorporated in August 1998. Onix is perhaps one of the first Māori private military and security companies operating from New Zealand. The company was owned by Ken Whatuira a former soldier from the NZSAS and British 22 SAS[1], Anthony Hauraki and Westland Ltd.[2] Westland Ltd was reported to be a debenture holder in Onix and to have a director from the Waipareira Trust on its board, which suggests money may have been loaned by the Waipareira Trust to Westland Ltd for Onix.[3]

The operation in Indonesia brought a great deal of media attention to Onix and may have been their first (and last) contract overseas as a company. New Zealand media reported that eight former SAS soldiers were involved in the rescue of a kidnapped man, Johnson Cornelius Lo or Roesli Hartono.[4] Hartono was reportedly from a wealthy Indonesian family.[5] John Tamihere was reported as saying about those involved that they had 'done exceptionally well in the military, and now as civilians provided "excellent VIP security" at home and abroad.'[6]

In 1998 Onix had a number of high profile contracts within New Zealand that have been reported about and possibly some overseas which are unknown. For the America's Cup race in 2000, Onix was contracted to protect the cup itself and provide close protection for Sir Peter Blake who had allegedly received death threats.[7] Nathan Hislop, who worked for Onix in 2000, has stated that after the America's Cup the number of jobs inside New Zealand dwindled so many of the people working for the company, like himself, went to Iraq to work.[8] Former SAS soldier and television personality Barrie Rice also allegedly worked for Onix before going to Iraq.

The reduction in the number of jobs available within New Zealand may have also made it more difficult for Onix to continue operating. In addition, as with any industry the failure of those individuals or companies that contract the work to pay on time (or at all) can prove fatal for a business. On 12 December 2000 the High Court in Auckland placed Onix into liquidation and in December 2002 the liquidator produced a final report indicating that it was unable to locate any assets and therefore no creditors could be paid.[9] The timing of these financial issues and anecdotal evidence suggests that whoever contracted Onix for the job in Indonesia did not pay and this led directly to the company's insolvency.

Another media report about Māori involved in private security work came in December 2006. New Zealander David Pemberton was arrested and charged by police in Lebanon after allegedly kidnapping two children, whose mother, it transpired, had contracted him to rescue them in a custody dispute.[10] Former SAS soldier Michael Rewi also allegedly assisted with the contract but escaped Lebanon.

Further attention to Māori involvement in the industry came from news of the deaths of at least three Māori being killed between 2006 and 2007 in Iraq and Afghanistan. Teina Ngamata, in 2006 and Darryl de Thierry in Iraq in July 2007.[11] Teina Ngamata was an ex-soldier from Rarotonga, living in Waikato who had been working for ArmourGroup since 2004.[12] De Thierry had previously served in the New Zealand military and worked in Iraq for ArmourGroup.[13] Like other Māori in the industry he had relocated to Australia two years before. In December 2007 there were also reports of another Māori based in Australia, Kelly Clark, having been killed in Afghanistan.[14]

Very little is known about the numbers of injuries or deaths of people working in the privatised military industry or associated occupations. The first reported case of a New Zealander being killed while working in Iraq was the death of John Robert Tyrrell.[15] Tyrrell was an engineer and prime minister of the day Helen Clark offered her condolences to the family.[16] Tyrrell's death was the only death in Iraq for which Helen Clark did offer her condolences. Was it because he was an engineer rather than in a security or combat role? New Zealanders working as operators in the industry were killed between 2006 and 2007 but no press releases were issued from the Beehive to mark their passing. These inconsistencies in the reporting and acknowledgement of some deaths, but not others, make it even more difficult to get a clear picture of the industry.

In July 2007 Willie Apiata was announced as the recipient of a Victoria Cross medal. This drew media attention to Māori in the military and also led to further interest in Māori in faraway places. In September 2007 TV3 screened a documentary called *Soldiers of Fortune* featuring Barrie Rice, a former SAS member returning to do one last contract in Iraq.

Since 2007 there have been very few media reports about Māori in the privatised military industry and those which have appeared have often been linked to other more local events or conversations. In 2012 the final trials were held for people who had been arrested in the 2007 'Operation 8' raids conducted by the police on Māori and non-Māori environmental and sovereignty activists. It became public that Rau Hunt, a former navy petty officer and allegedly someone who had worked in the privatised military industry in Iraq, had presented evidence for the defendants regarding whether or not he had been training them for security work in Iraq.[17] There was some dispute about whether he had merely been showing them the kinds of tactics used for close protection scenarios and how to protect people or whether he was demonstrating and training them how to take hostages – skills which allegedly they might have been going to use for 'terrorism' in New Zealand.[18] This connection raised an issue that was not well discussed subsequently about why, with so many Māori serving in the military, there had not previously been attempts by Māori to pursue sovereignty issues with military means. That conversation is still to be had.

In 2013 a story about Hemi Anisi's involvement in maritime security was printed in *The New Zealand Herald*[19] but did not specifically discuss his Māori heritage. *He Toki Huna*, a film produced by Annie Goldson and Kay Ellmers for Māori Television in 2013 explored New Zealand involvement in Afghanistan. It featured comments from a Māori former soldier, Alpha Kennedy who left the New Zealand military to work for a New Zealand company, International Strategic Development Solutions, with contracts in Afghanistan.

Media reports of de Thierry's death in 2007 made mention of the fact that '2,000 New Zealanders, mostly with military or police backgrounds' had taken contracts to work in Iraq.[20] Despite the apparent numbers involved, following 2007 very little media attention has explored the presence of Māori in the industry. Moreover, that no more deaths have been reported since 2007 raises a number of worrying questions about the industry and reporting of it. What has happened for Māori in the intervening years? Estimates from interviews conducted for this book suggest that there are currently at least twenty-five Māori on maritime contracts (offshore) on the east coast of Africa alone. Globally there could be more than 200 Māori operators working on contracts. In the next section, five of these Māori provide their insights on the industry.

END NOTES

1. Dearnaley, 'Ex-SAS shocked,' March 2000.
2. New Zealand Companies Office website, accessed 28 June 2015, http://www.business.govt.nz/companies/app/ui/pages/companies/920127/shareholdings
3. Staff Reporters, 'Ex-SAS Men,' March, 2000.
4. Ibid.
5. M. Dearnaley, 'Papers tell of diplomat's rescue slipup,' *New Zealand Herald*, 19 April 2000, accessed 28 June 2015, http://www.nzherald.co.nz/nz/news/article.cfm?c_id=1&objectid=132197.
6. Staff Reporters, 'Ex-SAS Men,' March 2000.
7. J. Ash, 'Yachting, a Safer life with the cup yachts,' *New Zealand Herald*, 24 June 2006.
8. Ibid.
9. Ferrier Hodgson, 'Report on Liquidation' (Onix Report, 29 November 2002).

10 Radio New Zealand, 'Former NZ Soldier Reportedly Charged Over Lebanese Kidnapping,', 30December 2006.
11 S. O'Rourke, 'Grief Shatters Family Haven,' *New Zealand Herald*, 11 August 2006.
12 'New Zealander Killed in Iraq Farwelled in Packed Ceremony,' *New Zealand Herald*, 21 August 2006.
13 L. Cleave, 'Kiwi in Iraq died doing work he loved,' *New Zealand Herald*, 13 July 2007.
14 M. McPherson, 'Bay Security Guard Dies in Afghanistan War Zone,' *Bay of Plenty Times*, 15 December 2007.
15 B. Carter, 'Dead Man Ignored Family's Pleas,' *New Zealand Herald,* 12 May 2004.
16 Helen Clark, 'NZ Man Dies in Iraq' (Statement 11 May 2004), accessed 19 June 2014, http://www.beehive.govt.nz/node/19659
17 R. Hemara, 'Operation 8: Weaving the Police "Terrorism" Narrative', *Te Putatara,* November 2013.
18 E. Gay, 'Security Expert Denies Telling Urewera Four How to Take Hostages,' *New Zealand Herald*, March 7, 2012; G. Cumming and C. Masters, 'A Nation Divided: Inside the Urewera Four Trial,' *New Zealand Herald*, 24 March 2012; R. Hemara, 'Operation 8: Weaving the Police "Terrorism" Narrative,' *Te Putatara,* November 2013.
19 P. Charman, 'Kiwi sees fighting off pirates as just a job,' *New Zealand Herald*, 20 July 2013.
20 Cleave, 'Kiwi in Iraq,' July 2007.

PART TWO:
THE PEOPLE

LAND BASED SECURITY

Pictures of chunky, armed men against a backdrop of sand are one of the common images that people generate when thinking about people working for PMSCs. However, there are a wide range of roles for operators and these relate to the type of company that they are working for. Peter Singer argues there are three main categories of PMSCs, military provider firms, military consulting firms and military support firms.[1] Military provider companies provide operators that will be 'engaging in actual fighting, either as line units or specialists (for example, combat pilots) and/or direct command and control of field units'.[2] This may involve fighting to protect people (such as diplomats, media or engineers), or to protect or acquire assets (such as buildings or other infrastructure or specific resources like oil refineries). These types of activities are the privatised military industry's most controversial often because they involve the use of lethal force, as discussed earlier.[3] Operators working for a military consulting firm 'provide advisory and training services integral to the operation and restructuring of a client's armed forces ... they offer strategic, operational, and/or organizational analysis ... they do not operate on the battlefield itself'.[4] Finally, military support firms provide services that include 'non-lethal aid and assistance, including logistics, intelligence, technical support, supply and transportation'.[5]

The 2003 Iraq war began with the United States and a coalition of the United Kingdom, Australia and France invading Iraq to depose Saddam Hussein and allegedly look for, and disarm, weapons of mass destruction. Though the United States declared victory only two short months after the initial invasion, it is now apparent the presence of US and other military forces and US companies in Iraq has continued much longer.

Estimates suggest that although the 2003 ratio of US troops to private contractors was around ten to one, by 2010 this had increased to one to one,[6] starkly demonstrating the levels of privatisation since the 1990 Gulf War where the ratio was sixty to one.[7] The United States Government relied heavily upon private military and security companies to both support their initial actions and as they have begun to withdraw the numbers of their military in Iraq. As explained earlier, the PMSCs are involved in combat operations as well as logistics, and other supporting functions.

A number of large companies have dominated the US Department of Defense contracts for a range of military security services:[8] Kellogg, Brown and Root (KBR) – a former subsidiary of Halliburton – have been awarded by far the most contracts in Iraq with an estimated US$39.5billion in US federal contracts from 2003 to 2013.[9] Alongside KBR, other dominant companies have also earned in the (US) billions of dollars: DynCorp received US$4.1billion for training Iraqi police officers, Blackwater/Xe/Academi received US$1.3billion for security work and Triple Canopy received US$1.8billion, also for security work.[10]

Most of those employed as security contractors in Iraq in the first couple of years after 2003 were from special forces units, such as the New Zealand Special Air Service (NZSAS). Most of the personnel employed to engage in actual fighting are logically drawn from the military sector. Some companies have policies of only employing people from their own state military (such as MPRI) but others (such as ArmorGroup) are multinational.[11] As the war continued, however, this employment demographic began to change. Even though the US Department of Defense was contracting companies, PMSCs themselves had from the beginning relied less on United States citizens and more on 'third country nationals' (TCNs) or 'local nationals' (LNs) (in this case the 'local nationals' being from Iraq).

Although little specific information exists about the ethnicity of those employed under the US Department of Defense in the years 2003 to 2008 some information has been made available that dates from 2008. From analysing this information, Maya Eichler concludes that in 2011 in Iraq the US Department of Defense 'relied on close to 53,000 defence contractors of which 55% were TCNs and 15% were Iraqi citizens'[12] and out of the '9,554 security contractors in Iraq, 87% were TCNs and 4% locals'.[13] These numbers indicate that 'US citizens have made up only a relatively small percentage of employees hired under DoD contracts in Iraq and Afghanistan'.[14] One of the possible benefits of this situation for the US Department of Defense has been that the numbers of reported injuries and deaths of US citizens appears much lower than would be the case if the United States Government used its own citizens to continue in Iraq and Afghanistan.

Within the category of 'third country nationals' it is useful to consider three separate types of peoples that appear to exist in something of a hierarchy. There are those from the United Kingdom, Australia, South Africa, Canada and New Zealand where these special forces have some familiarity with the training and methods that each use. The next group could be described as from the 'global south', including countries like India, Pakistan and Chile. The third group are those from Eastern Europe and the former Soviet Union.[15] Māori are grouped as New Zealanders, or 'Kiwis'.

One of the reasons that New Zealanders have been so sought after is their reputation for fitting in easily with multinational teams. In his research, Blackwell argues that the New Zealand Army Special Operations unit is unique because as a result of its relatively small size, in terms of personnel and funding, 'personnel are trained to operate effectively alongside, or as a small contingent of, a larger multi-national force. This ability to integrate rapidly and effectively is seen as a key attribute by senior PMC managers'.[16]

There were a number of reasons for PMSCs changing whom they sought to employ. One reason was that PMSCs needed more personnel and there weren't enough special forces people to fulfil that need. As companies in search of profit, they could also see the potential to increase their profits if they could pay slightly lower – or much lower – wages.

Wages that were offered in the early part of the Iraq war were much higher than in more recent years and reflected the fact that the special forces operators were in high demand by PMSCs. Wages ranged from approximately US$300 to $1,000 per day. The conditions of contracts varied but most were for specific time periods and had some element of rotation where operators returned to their country of origin for several weeks (the intensity of this kind of work requires long breaks). At the end of each contract many operators would pack up and travel back to their country of origin without knowing whether they would have more work or not.[17]

One of the consequences of PMSCs using 'third country nationals' or 'local nationals' was that many of the special forces operators no longer wanted to work in units where the skills and training of those around them was significantly different to theirs, or where they were unsure of the standard, potentially putting them at risk in combat situations. For many operators, the amount of money they were earning no longer balanced with the risks they were taking. Blackwell found that one of the aspects of privatised military contracting that New Zealand personnel he interviewed *least liked* 'was the [lower] calibre of some of the other people being employed by private companies … The "gold rush" in Iraq where numerous firms entered the market that were either new to the business or had expanded rapidly to meet demand, has resulted in a lowering of the standards of the contractors being employed'.[18]

In the next section I outline the experiences of a Māori operator who worked for PMSCs based on the land and who shares his stories about the industry.

T (TE ĀTIAWA, NGĀTI KAHUNGUNU)

As an ex-NZSAS soldier T entered Iraq alongside many other former special forces operators in 2003.

T had left the NZSAS in 1995. With a friend he went to Hanoi looking for work in the private security industry. Attending an oil and gas symposium they found that they were in over their heads and decided that the work that was available there was not for them. After consulting with other friends about potential work, T and his mate ended up in Cambodia.

> Yeah, we went to Hanoi with a few expectations and found it wasn't what we expected at all. B knew an ex-unit member who was working out of Tanzania so he gave him a call to see if there was any work for us there.

No, was the answer to that question. However, he did give us a telephone number of a friend of his who was working out of Phnom Penh, and so we gave his friend a call and 'lo and behold', next day we were both off on a plane to Cambodia.

I didn't mind Cambodia at all; in fact, I quite liked it. It wasn't for everyone though. I didn't mind the poverty we were living in. Well, it wasn't 'abject poverty' – nothing like what the locals were living in, but it wasn't flash either. I enjoyed the country, enjoyed the food and enjoyed the various activities that Phnom Penh had to offer at that time. Work was pretty sporadic, we had a couple of odd jobs here and there doing different stuff but Cambodia in '96 was still relatively unstable.

The UN [United Nations] had come in and had 'stabilised' the country to a point where, in 1993, they were able to conduct national elections. However, the result of the elections was questioned by one of the losing parties who then threatened to take Cambodia back into a state of war. And so, to maintain stability, a 'two-government' system was implemented. Yeah, like that was really gonna work, ay. Basically you had two governments who officially 'shared power' but unofficially were at each other's throats – literally. The Funcinpec Party (led by Norodom Ranariddh) was a royalist party, and I think they had come out on top after the '93 elections. The CPP [Cambodian People's Party] (under Hun Sen) was the other main party and they had governed Cambodia since the late seventies early eighties, after the Khmer Rouge (KR) had been displaced from most of the big towns and cities, and didn't take too kindly to them coming second in the elections. Then you had the KR, they didn't even want to take part in any election, and carried on 'doing what they always did' in the various districts where they still had strongholds.

So the country, or its population, was generally split into three groups – nah, make that four groups if you count the thousands of people who chose to become refugees. Anyway, two of those groups were strong political parties whilst the third was a group who didn't want to recognise the power and/or status that the other two had. All of them had guns, some had artillery, some of them even had tanks, but they all had one thing in common, they all wanted to be the boss. And this was the environment we were going into with the hope of getting work.

While T assumed that there would be hundreds of security jobs in a situation like this he found the reality quite different.

I guess for a country to offer up the opportunities for jobs in the security industry you gotta have a few things in place. First of all, there needs to be a security risk. Hmm, obviously. However, it must be a security risk of a certain level – if it's too low, then there is no need to hire people for security. Funnily enough though, if it's too high, then there's not much work around 'cause you're probably working in a 'war zone', and generally, the only guys who you'll find working there are the 'soldiers' who are fighting for one side or the other.

Cambodia probably had the right level of risk, but it was missing one key factor: it didn't really have natural resources that were highly sought after and were readily available in large quantities. Because with those large-scale, readily available valuable natural resources comes the commercial prospect of making money – large amounts of money. Now, couple that with poorly enforced fiscal regulations – or there is no regulatory framework at all due to instability in the government – then you basically have a burly bomb that starts to attract multi-billion dollar companies out looking to make an easy million or two. And so, they send out work crews to get in first and establish themselves, and it's in this slightly chaotic environment where you can pick up good paying security work with well-established reputable international companies.

Unfortunately, Cambodia didn't have large amounts of oil, or gas, or gold, or copper or much else. Yeah, they had lots of hardwood forests, but the KR had a stranglehold on that trade to the north-west whilst the Vietnamese had a stranglehold on the trade to the north-east. Cambodia had land, vast amounts of arable land, but in terms of gold, oil, gas or anything – nah, it just wasn't there.

So the oil and gas companies, the huge construction companies, they weren't there either. Well, they weren't there in great numbers – they weren't rushing in – and it's those kinds of companies that provide work for the security contractors, those are the people that hire you, and they just weren't there. Oh sure, if you knew the right person, or worked for the right company, Cambodia offered a real cruisy job with regards to security, but we didn't know the right people and we didn't work for the right company – in fact, we didn't work at all.

T got a job in Brunei then returned to Cambodia and eventually back to New Zealand to work for his Rūnanga on environmental management. He participated in discussions with the regional council about an 'ocean policy' and management of the coastline and harbour areas but found this kind of work wasn't really for him and returned to Cambodia. In Cambodia T helped support the development of local rugby competitions for kids. And he even helped out on a movie set.

In May, June and July 2003 T was getting many emails from mates suggesting he join them in Iraq.

I wasn't doing anything in particular. I was back in New Zealand at the time, just chilling out really. Anyway, I got a phone call from L, a mate of mine, who told me to go and see another ex-member, a guy who was recruiting for CRG (Control Risk Group) at the time, and before I knew it, I was booked on a flight to England with L with a job lined up for me in Basra. Simple as that. There was no real interview or anything, it was basically just 'do you have a passport and when can you leave?' It really was a case of who you know or who knew you.

Yeah, I guess in the end, you had to have a CV to at least fulfil the company's basic requirements and to ensure they got the details right on your payslip, but that wasn't what got you through the door, it was the fact that someone in the 'right place' knew you and could vouch for you. And of course, being ex-squadron, there was a high chance that the guys who knew you were already in the 'right places' within the company.

So yeah, we turned up, signed up, jumped on a plane and left. Hmm, I think we left in August or September 2003. I can't really remember now, I know we ended up over in Basra. Quite hard case really, I flew in on a plane full of Brits but when we got to the camp in Basra, what struck me was the number of Kiwis who were there, and what struck me even more was that I knew 99 percent of them. There were like twenty or thirty of us there, almost all ex-army, mostly ex-grunts, quite a few ex-squadron. The only odd ones out were an engineer, an armourer and a couple of the ex-Kiwi cops. Oh yeah, and one Kiwi cop who was over there on leave …

Yeah, so in terms of private security companies that was the start of it for me. I worked there from 2003 and my last job was 2005 or 2006. Yeah, once again, can't remember exactly when.

Like many other former special forces soldiers, for T the route into the industry and Iraq was clearly through personal connections.

… Yeah, in the beginning, a whole lot of ex-Kiwi soldiers scored jobs over there through, or by, word of mouth. So if you had mates involved in work over there, it made it a whole lot easier to get a job. Which was one of the good things about having served in the NZSAS, cause bro, there were ex-squadron members all over the world. A lot of them are well established in the security industry and a lot of them have really good connections. So yeah, if you know the right guy you can sorta bypass certain routes to get in. If say, you were looking for a job with a particular company and just happened to have a mate who knew you, then sometimes it was just a case of saying, 'Mate, got any work on?' And sometimes the answer was, 'Yep. OK, come over.'

Yeah man, it's not what you know, it's who you know … and I guess that's because at the end of the day that's the only real way a company can know what the new person is like. Like I said before, you can write anything in a CV, but having someone who knows you, that's real, and if that person who knows you is a trusted person within the organisation, then they're more than likely to accept you or offer you a job.

Reputation of your parent unit plays a part in this. If you've been a badged member with the NZSAS or some other special force groups (Brit SAS, Aussie SASR, Delta, Navy Seals and other well-known units) your chances of scoring a job are pretty damn good. And because no one really trusts anyone else outside their unit, you find 'like attracts like', and so Kiwis hire Kiwis, Aussies hire Aussies, Brits hire Brits (unless it's a low-paying contract, then they'll hire Kiwis and Aussies) and of course, Americans hire Americans. That's not saying you can't get a job with anyone outside your nationality, no way, it just made it easier if you served with the guys who worked for the company you want a job with. So yeah, you end up trusting your mates and/or those guys who your mates can vouch for and the flow-on effect is that the more guys you work with the more guys you learn to trust, or not trust, as the case may be. Once again, seeing something written on paper counts for shit. Anyone can write a story, some people do and have done in the past, so the only real way of knowing is to ask around the guys who have worked on the circuit.

T would travel in and out of Iraq in a number of ways over the next years.

If you're working in Iraq then there are multiple entry/exit points, it all depended on which part of Iraq you worked in. Not everyone flew in and out of the BIAP (Baghdad International Airport). Yeah sure, if you worked in and around Baghdad then the route in and out was generally through the BIAP. But you know, you could drive out through to Kuwait in the south or go way up north to Turkey through the Zakho border crossing. You could even drive out through to Jordan, but that meant having to go through Fallujah and Ramadi, and foreigners weren't exactly welcome in those neighbourhoods, although I did hear of a couple of American security contractors who decided to 'hang' around Fallujah a while.

My first flight though, was in through the APOD [Aerial Port of Debarkation] in Basra and that was from Brize Norton [Royal Air Force Base, Oxfordshire], but that was a one-off. However, when working other contracts in the south we generally drove out through the land border with Kuwait. After Basra I got sent up to Kirkuk and then up to Erbil which is in the far north of Iraq. Erbil was cool 'cause we stayed at this real flash hotel, The Khanzad I think was its name. Man, the food was good, the beds were comfortable and the women up there had everything a man could want – long hair, big muscles and a moustache. We were actually trying to get flights out of Erbil, but never managed it. Apparently they got it up and running later on and the airport there is now a bit of a regional hub, but no, for us to get out of Erbil we had to drive all the way back down to Baghdad. Yeah, that was fun – not!

So yeah, where you entered and exited Iraq generally depended on where you worked or where you got debriefed. So for the first company I worked with, the main base was Baghdad, and at some point in time you all had to come back across the country into Baghdad and whether it was to have a discussion with management, upgrade your skills through a bit of training, get updates on intel or whatever, it was always good to catch up with all the other guys in your company to see what was happening in their locations. 'Cause I tell ya, some people never ever got to see anybody else; they just stayed out in their regions and left from their respective locations. Mate, so long as they did their job and reported back, the company was happy. I guess when you have access to the Internet, email, cell phones, you don't really have to go and see people in person and besides, quite often the security threat levels were so high it was unadvisable to be on the roads anyway.

In fact, yeah, there was a situation in Easter 2004 when the south erupted and there was no way that anyone (apart from the locals) were moving on the roads. It seems Muqtada al-Sadr and the Mahdi army were flexing their muscles and creating mayhem for coalition forces in the southern regions. For a few of my mates who were based out at Nasiriyah at the time, they reckoned it was like 'Fort Apache'. They were stuck in a compound surrounded by blast walls while the locals were driving up and down the main road firing their AK's and shooting rockets at them. Apparently this went on day and night for quite a while and the Italian *Carabinieri* who were based there with them got so tired that they let some of our guys man the .50 cal [.50 calibre gun] they had set up on the roof.

Another one of our groups based in Al-Kut were in a similar position. They got absolutely hammered by RPGs, don't ask me how nobody in the base got killed during those attacks but someone must've said some pretty powerful prayers.

During that particular time period there was generally no stability/security and driving on the roads was pretty much off-limits for us ... unless you had a military escort and even then sometimes the military escort attracted trouble instead of deterring it.

At that time, our role was to protect people working for the British Government. Not high-ranking diplomats or anything but people who were there to try and re-establish some semblance of order around the place. They may have been there to ascertain the level of damage to infrastructure or try to put back in place some form of municipal or authoritarian management. Some of the guys we looked after were just trying to solve the freshwater supply problem, some the power/electrical supply to various centres, some the schooling and education issues. But whatever they were there for, and no matter what positive humanitarian aid they were providing as a consequence, what I gathered was that they were there to rebuild the infrastructure to a point where it would facilitate the flow of oil out of the country.

Anyway, there was this one lady and she was based up in Erbil. Apparently, she had worked in various Arabic countries and was quite the specialist in understanding the Middle East. I just think she thought she knew it all. Anyway, she had to go out on leave and insisted on going out through Mosul. And if you thought Baghdad was bad, Mosul was worse. This is only my perspective, but to me Mosul was a big 'turf war' between gangs – you had Shia Arabs, Sunni Arabs, you had the poor old locals who had lived there forever and a day and then you had the Kurds, and they were all scrapping over control of their part of Mosul.

Regarding the Kurds, Mosul may not be as politically important to them as Erbil or Kirkuk, but they knew that Mosul was strategically important because it was the gateway into Europe. All the trucks carrying all the supplies/goods/oil would come up through the main highway and go through Mosul, then go on out to a place called Zakho (controlled by the Kurds) and then across the border to Silopi, which is in Turkey – and Turkey was the gateway to Europe – that was the land bridge for goods, supplies, everything. We were up at Zakho one time and we looked across the border towards Turkey and there was a traffic jam 13 kilometres long. There was this one continuous line of trucks all the way in.

So it was a huge strategically important place and you had the Arabs, Shia and Sunni, fighting each other. You had the old locals and you had the Kurds and they were (at some time or another) fighting each other – mate, it was just one big mess. And to cap it off, you had the Americans who were fighting everyone while at the same time trying to keep the peace. Yeah right!

Yep, the best thing about doing a run into Mosul was getting the fuck out of there as soon as you could. Our guys got hit twice when I was up there, so no one, nobody, really wanted to drive in and out and fair enough too.

So yeah, I got made the boss one time and here was this lady who wanted to fly out of Mosul to go on leave. She could have gone down to Baghdad or even down to Kirkuk and flown out of the main camp there, but no, she wanted to show the various groups who were threatening the coalition [US Coalition] that she wasn't going to bend or buckle under the threats made to her life, and she was going to fly out of Mosul. Yeah, well maybe *she* wanted to, but nobody else did and she wasn't going to get to Mosul with one of *our* security details driving her there. So I said, 'No, I'm not going to risk a crew to drive you in to Mosul.' I then sought support from management down in Baghdad and in the end they got her a US military helicopter to fly from Erbil to Mosul. Which I scratched my head at 'cause those choppers were generally on immediate standby as medevac for the coalition forces. Bro, just imagine if a US soldier required an immediate medevac and they had to say 'no, sorry mate. You can't have this chopper to come and save your life because this lady wants to go home on leave through Mosul.'

As is commonly acknowledged, personnel were there largely for the money and moved companies accordingly. T had registered a company in Hong Kong and was a 'non-resident' based outside of New Zealand for tax purposes to maximise the income he was receiving and he also picked companies depending on the wages being offered.

> My mate's still on about US$800 a day. But he's working in Abu Dhabi now, maybe he's on more, maybe he's on less now, I don't know. They've got different roles, different contracts. Yeah, me and a few mates, we all started off together, all doing the same job or something similar and all on the same pay. We all worked together, and as we worked we got more experienced in the role, more experienced in the country and more experienced in the way that things worked over there with regards to the security industry. But the most important thing was that we made more contacts. Like I said before, it's not what you know, but who you know and before long, guys were jumping ship from one company to another.

> The working conditions weren't that much of an issue for me. It didn't bother me where we slept or what food we ate, or whether you had air con or Internet. I was just there to make money. It was an issue for other people though, and fair enough too. No matter where you were, there was always a chance of getting shot, getting mortared, getting hit by a roadside bomb or even having a rocket land on you or near you. So yeah, for some guys, having access to a hot meal was a big deal. So yeah, there was a variety of choices out there and it paid to shop around.

> How easy was it to switch companies? Fucking easy was the answer to that one. One day one of my mates asked me if I would consider switching

companies. He basically tapped me on the shoulder and said, 'Hey bey, you want to come work for us?' 'Oh yeah, what have you got to offer?' 'Four hundred pound a day.'

So I said OK. In saying that though, I quickly started doing my background checks by ringing around and asking my other mates what the company was like, who was running it, how good were they, what methods were they using, what weapons they had etcetera and that was it. One week later I was working for them – just jumped ship, just like that. Was it an easy decision? Yeah, well, at the time I was only on about $300 or so, and that's not money to be laughed at, but when a guy says we'll give you £400 a day, I kinda went 'Oh, OK, yep.'

So yeah, it was a different company and we operated differently. Some things were better, some things weren't as good, but overall, I liked the way they worked – low profile as opposed to high profile. It does have its risks, but it suited me.

T discovered that not only was money a priority for operators, but also the companies that employed them. In around 2005 wages in Iraq began to drop significantly as companies began to employ more 'third country nationals' who worked for less, but were not as well trained as those from western country special forces, such as the NZSAS. Huge companies like Blackwater (Xe, now Academi) began using former soldiers and police officers from Colombia who they paid as low as US$34 per day.[19]

... unfortunately there are always people who are willing to work cheaper. I think for the companies who hired the cheap labour it was a decision based on the financial aspects of operating over there – it sure as hell wasn't based on health and safety reasons.

So yeah, some companies hired them and paid the price through an increase in vehicle damage, injuries and deaths. At the same time though, other companies hired them and didn't suffer any more or any less. So for some companies it was just a calculated gamble they were prepared to take, and it was all about the money. They didn't really care about the guy who's out there doing the mahi and as much as they want to say they care about you, it really is all about the bottom line.

Yeah, we were in Basra one time, and we heard about this incident up in Baghdad. A vehicle with four persons in it was heading back into the Green Zone, coming up on one of the bridges, when a guy drove past and detonated a large bomb inside the car, and at the time of the explosion they were on an overpass. Anyway, the bomb was that big that it lifted the vehicle the guys were in and threw it over the side of the overpass and it fell about 70 feet. We think they may have survived the blast but died due to rapid deceleration injuries when the vehicle crashed into the ground. We also heard that the bodies were going to be put on a Hercules to be repatriated back to Britain and that it was coming to Basra on its way back. Anyway, some of the guys in our company had worked for that company and asked if they could go out to the airfield and pay their respects to the bodies. Being mainly British, our company had no problems agreeing to that and helped to facilitate not only the ex-company members working for us, but also any other ex-company members working around the Basra area who knew the guys who died.

So the guys went out to the airbase, the Herc came in, the guys went out onto the tarmac, the ramp came down and the loadie said to the guys: 'We'll bring the coffins out so you guys can have a quick service for your mates.' So the loadie pulled one coffin out, then another coffin out and then another coffin out, and the guys were sitting there on the ramp waiting for the fourth coffin. Waiting, waiting ... And the loadie goes: 'Oh that's all there is.' Say what?! 'Nah there's only three coffins, mate.' 'But there were four guys who were killed. The families back in England are gonna be expecting four coffins.'

Yeah, well, apparently the company didn't want to, or didn't think it was worth buying four coffins seeing as the bodies were basically mincemeat so they stuck four bodies into three coffins. Boy, those ex-company dudes were furious. So they went out and bought another coffin and took body parts from the other three and made up a *fourth body*. They also gave instructions advising that the coffins not be opened on arrival in England. Yeah, it was all about the money. Why didn't they buy a fourth coffin? Oh, 'cause it cost too much.

While life-threatening situations were regular occurrences for T and other operators it is extremely difficult to find accurate statistics on the numbers of people who do lose their lives in the industry. Some statistics from the United States suggest that between June 2009 and March 2011, contractor deaths in Iraq and Afghanistan, including local and third country nationals, exceeded the military's deaths in both countries.[20] 'Moreover, contractor deaths are undoubtedly higher than the reported total because federal statistics are based on filed insurance claims, and many foreign contractors' employees may be unaware of their insurance rights and therefore unlikely to file for compensation'.[21]

There was a time when we were in Baghdad when the run to the BIAP was like 'running the gauntlet'. Like, you know, jump on the road, toss the coin, roll the dice, whatever – some days you lose and some days you win. Some days the 'bad guys' shot at you, some days the Americans shot at you. It didn't really make any difference how good, how highly skilled you were, it was just a case of rolling the dice and hoping your number doesn't come up.

People were dying every day on that section of highway due to insurgent attacks, and it got that serious that the big companies who hired the security companies all got together and were actually thinking about buying their own tanks, bringing in their own army to run patrols along the BIAP. Yeah, not everyone could afford the helicopter ride from the airport to the Green Zone, but even those people who could afford to fly still needed to secure the highway, to secure this particular stretch of road as it was the life-blood of the IZ, or the 'International Zone'. The IZ is just another name given to the Green Zone, and this was where all the big foreign companies operated out of, or where they had their headquarters. So yeah, this one little stretch of road was really important. As for how many people lost their lives on that stretch of road – that's a question only Allah and Jesus can answer. Maybe you can ask them for their tally sheets one day.

Between 2003 and 2007 around 700,000 weapons were imported into Iraq by the United States for the Iraqi security forces for them to assist the US forces with fighting and 'retaining law and order'.[22] In 2005 'the US entity responsible for their distribution could not account for 110,000 AK-47 rifles, 80,000 pistols, 135,000 items of body armour and 115,000 helmets – more than 50 per cent of all the equipment'.[23] Some may have been 'lost in the system'[24] but others were destined for market. T found that some operators and companies did buy their weapons locally because at times companies either didn't have their own weapons or their reliability was questionable.

> We had to go out and buy our own, one time. So one of our managers went down to the local market with one of the locals and they bought a whole lot of AK-47s. But these weren't Russian made, these were Pakistani made, or locally made, some might have been Chinese, we don't know where they came from. So we had to go through all these weapons and sort them out into working lots – as in these ones work, these ones don't. We then had to go through all the working parts of each weapon and make sure the serial numbers matched, then we took them down the range and fired them. So yeah, it was a little bit of an effort to sort all that stuff out. But if you really think about it, that weapon could save your life one day.

> Initially our weapons were locally sourced, but later on the company bought some better stuff. And yes, what weapons you got depended on who you worked for and what 'profile' they were running. One company adopted the 'porcupine' profile where they had flat-deck trucks, modified SUVs and utes with sandbagged sides, twin gimpys [general purpose machine gun] mounted on the rear, vehicle-mounted .30 or .50 cals [calibre gun], all sticking out like the spines on a porcupine. I don't know if 'porcupine' is an actual type of profile but it fits the description pretty well. Basically they had lots of guns, and it seemed like lots of Fijians worked for

them as well. That was them – very, very high profile. They said 'here we are, attack us if you dare'. But that was the way they chose to operate. So in terms of sourcing weapons, I dare say those would have been sourced in the States – flown over. They had the money to do that.

Some guys used to buy, or 'acquire' their own weapons because the stuff they issued you with wasn't up to standard. Lots of guys modified their own weapons and equipment: modified their own holsters, modified their body armour, their vehicles, everything really. So you could either use the stuff which the company gave you or you could go out and source your own. Some companies provided really good equipment for their guys, some just gave out a load of crap; it was *your* choice whether you wanted to work for the company, it was your choice whether you wanted to use their equipment. You could always go out and get your own stuff; it was just a matter of money.

For T, being Māori in Iraq mattered in some contexts but not in others. It helped to connect with Māori and other New Zealanders and at other times was a connection with local Iraqis.

Being Māori in Iraq is a moot point really. As far as the rest of the world is concerned Māoris are Kiwis and over there, you are identified as a Kiwi first before anything else. And yeah, as a Kiwi you hung out with other Kiwis, some were Māori, some were Pākehā, some were Tongan, some Samoan. Lots were Fijian, well, not Fijian Kiwis, we just used to hang out with the Fijians 'cause they liked playing touch [rugby] – same as the Aussies.

Anyway, with regards to being a security contractor, being Māori was irrelevant. What was important was how professional you were. It didn't matter what race you were. If you were professional at doing your job over there you generally earned respect from other guys. Maybe your race/colour might have extended the time before you became accepted/ respected but one way to speed up that acceptance is to do well when you are under fire. Bullets are some of the most un-biased, non-racist things in the world – they will kill anyone of any colour no matter what their religion and when people are under stress, they don't care what colour/race of person comes to rescue them.

Your connections or your nationality might get you into Iraq, but once you get over there, it comes down to how you operate that stands you apart and soon enough, within your little group, you begin to find out who you can trust and who you can't, who you want to go out on the road with and who you don't want to go out on the road with.

Yeah, there are lots of Māori in this industry over in Iraq and Afghanistan. That's a consequence, I guess, of the high proportion of Māori who choose to join the army. They end up in different units, do their time in the army, get bored or get out and they become prime candidates for this role. Yeah, it's probably more the fact that you're a Kiwi soldier rather than you're a Māori.

Kiwis work well together over there because we generally understand each other. Just as Brits understand other Brits, Aussies understand other Aussies, etcetera ... But it seems Kiwis can get on with others, whereas the Brits don't tend to mix too well with the Americans, while the Aussies seem to have a grudge against the Brits dating back to the Second World War. But you know what? When the shit hits the fan, we're all mates. In the long run, the decision over who you choose to work with (that's if you have a choice) comes down to personality and skill level – because at the end of the day it's your life that is on the line.

So yeah, in this industry, race/nationality didn't really matter, skills mattered more.

One of the areas that T found Māori were different was in relation to getting to know the locals and their customs – the type of information companies often didn't provide.

Now, after saying all that, it's not so much being 'a Māori' that gives you a point of difference, rather it's being brought up 'as 'Māori' that may be of assistance to getting work or helping you in your work, especially when working in foreign countries where locals don't speak English and don't share recognisable customs and beliefs.

Yeah, because growing up in large whānau (communal) groups teaches you at a very young age how to work together with others. You may not like your cousins, but you all, at some stage, have to do the dishes in the marae, have to clean up after a hui, sweep the floor of the wharenui, put the mats away, put the mattresses away, stack all the chairs, maybe go hunting with your uncles, peel spuds in the kitchen, help dig the hāngi pit, help shuck the pāua, shell the mussels, shuck the kina. Yum! Try to sleep in the wharenui when everyone is snoring, play touch outside on the marae ātea and getting told off by your uncles, aunties or other kaumātua for playing there, sing waiata, do a haka, perform pōhiri for manuhiri. You end up doing all these things and all these things become part of you and you learn, you learn that there are many different types of personalities within your whānau and outside your whānau and at some point, you have to/need to work with them. Otherwise its gonna be a very, very long day working by yourself trying to cut the gorse/blackberry out the back of the farm if you piss them off and they go help someone else.

It is through these experiences that you develop an understanding of people and sometimes, it is this understanding that makes you comfortable in dealing with strangers, dealing with manuhiri, or simply dealing with guys who do things slightly differently to you. It helps you fit in easier and you're able to make others feel more comfortable working with you. You learn that different groups of people have different kawa and tikanga relating to everyday activities and you learn to be respectful of those differences.

That's probably one of the differences between Kiwis (I include Pākehā Kiwis in this group) and other foreign nationals. Kiwis generally took more time to learn the local way of doing things, we took the time to talk to the locals and find out what they do and don't do, what upsets people and what you do to not upset people. Always ask. Some of the locals we asked were honest with their replies and some guys weren't. Some didn't trust us and some we didn't trust, but you had to try to at least develop a safe working relationship. Which reminds me of this one guy – W.

Because of W and his friends, I now have a personal preference for working with the Iraqi Shia in Baghdad and Basra. That is not to say that the Sunni are not good to work with but I enjoyed working with W and his mates.

W was one of the locals who our company employed when I was working out of Baghdad. At that time, Muqtada al-Sadr was creating turmoil down south seemingly in a bid to raise his profile amongst his followers and perhaps convince others to switch allegiances to him. Muqtada al-Sadr was a Shia cleric, and a very well-known one as well, however he did not enjoy the following of the majority of Shia in Iraq. Anyway, one day our PSD [personal security detail] team had a job with the federal reserve dudes who were looking to help sort out the banking system, and our job was to run them into the central bank in Baghdad and then run them back to the Green Zone. I remember I was sitting down outside the bank having a break and I was talking to W about the events happening in his country and asked why Muqtada was causing trouble in the south.

W was saying: 'Don't worry, he's just a boy; he's living off the reputation of his father, how strong his father was.' W didn't believe in suicide bombings and said it was terrible thing to do, then he goes on to tell me about another imam, Ali al-Sistani. He says that this man is a great imam and is very wise and believes the end to the conflict is through politics, not through guns. And then he says to me: 'But 'T', if the imam he asks me to strap the bomb, I have to strap the bomb, but I will tell you first and then you can go away and then I will blow the bomb. OK?' Well, at least he was honest. And thanks for offering to give me a warning W – *cher* brother.

That was a display of their devotion to that particular person, that's how devoted they were. But at least he and his friends were honest, good, straight-up guys who worked well, and worked hard. They shared the same dangers as us but not the same money; they had to live outside the Green Zone and were under threat from others who resented them working for the coalition forces, and all because they needed to make a living to feed their families. One of his crew actually got hit by shrapnel from a roadside bomb that was targeting our vehicle. On that day W had sent him out on foot, well before we left the Green Zone, to check out likely ambush points, when a vehicle fitting the same description as ours turned down the street that led to the central bank.

So we were in Baghdad, which was dominated by Sunni at the time except for Sadr City. The Shia who worked for us lived under threat as well. So for them to be working for a foreign company was an extra risk. They knew that if certain people found out about what they did, they would be targeted for working for the infidels. A few of their families got killed and a few of their mates got shot. That was their reality, for them it was just another way to make a living for their families.

Guys from different countries treated them like crap as well and as a result, they didn't get much help. So it's all about understanding: understanding people, understanding cultural differences, understanding the language, that's where I think being Māori or being raised within a Māori environment made it easier for me to fit in with these guys. Māori weren't the only ones though, the Fijians were really good, they could speak multiple languages and were used to the communal lifestyle shared by the local population. Some of them spoke Hindi. Some of them spoke (obviously) Fijian, English and different languages. Because there were so many third country nationals over there from Bangladesh, Pakistan, some Fijians picked up languages left, right and centre, they were really good guys to work with.

T found that there were lots of Māori there at that time.

When I was there, there were at least eighty of us I think. Well, maybe eighty, maybe sixty, I don't know, nobody took a census count, but that was 2005. There could have been more, and that was only in Iraq. You've probably got a similar amount operating over in Afghan now. Yeah mate, Kiwis are all over the place and a good percentage of those will be Māori.

T found that one of the significant challenges in the private sector is not being able to rely on the extensive resources and assets of a state military. However, he also discovered that the connections that people maintain with their former colleagues can be the key.

When you're working in the industry you have no real backup. You're out there by yourself, just you and your team and you can't rely on anyone else. You can't call in an air strike, you can't ask for artillery support, you can't ask for a helo extract – well, not unless you work for a rich company.

... We had this issue in Al-Kut when one of the compounds our guys were at came under constant RPG fire; these guys were under serious threat and if they didn't get out of there they were going to die. We were trying to get assistance from the US Air Force, we were trying to get assistance from the Brits, we were trying to get assistance from the Americans. Apparently it was in a Polish sector but the military force in charge of security for the compound were Romanian. So yeah, no one was looking to risk their military assets to assist a private security company. In the end, the Romanians decided to make a break for it, so our guys and everyone else in the compound simply jumped in their vehicles and followed the Romanian APCs [armoured personnel carriers] out of there.

As for depending on your mates for help, well here's a good story; you can believe it or not. At the time that Al-Kut was under siege, I was in a command centre back in Baghdad. I had been asking around for help from the US dudes who were in there but they were saying that because it was a Polish-run sector they needed to get clearance before they could operate in the area or something like that. I was in there because I was the operations manager for that particular area. Also in there was another dude who was my counterpart for the American security company who also had guys stuck in Al-Kut.

We were both requesting support from any and all quarters and all the support was being denied. And now that I think about it, why should a military force support a civilian commercial company if it's not of tactical or strategic importance? Anyway, what it came down to was that us, as a civilian company, couldn't request US military air support, or British air support or British military support. We're just a private security company. So I saw this American dude from the other company wander over to the huge map of the area on the wall. He was looking at some of the detail on the map and chatting on his phone. As I got closer, I could hear him giving out what I recognised was a fire mission as he was giving figures and descriptions in a military format. And so I go to him: 'Bro, who you talking to?' 'Oh, just one of my buddies.' 'Oh, OK. Sounded like a fire mission to me.' He didn't answer. But he smiled.

So anyway, once our guys finally got back to Baghdad, I sat down with them and they debriefed me about the incident. They said they were taking a lot of rubbish from the locals and were getting low on ammo. The Romanians didn't want to come up on the roofs and help fight and that the only other people offering up resistance were the dudes from the US security company based at the other end of the compound. So yeah, they were taking a real hammering when all of a sudden they see these explosions over in the distance. Then they hear a humming noise up in the sky and suddenly a couple more explosions go off a little bit closer to them. The humming noise continues for a few more minutes and every now and then an explosion erupts on the ground. The PSD commander figures out that it must be an AC-130 [gunship]; they couldn't see it, but they could hear it and soon after that everything kinda went quiet.

My only guess is that the guy in the operations room had a mate who was still serving, and somehow he got his mate to provide his mates on the ground with a little bit of air support. That's how things happened. Yeah. That's why it's good to have friends.

Between contracts T travelled back to Cambodia.

> So when I was working in the industry, what did I do between jobs? I played rugby. I got back over to Cambodia and I got myself into rugby. But that was for the kids and helping stuff out and it was satisfying because it was an occupation where I was giving back. Helping people out rather than just exploiting them. Because at the end of the day the security companies are just living off the backs of those companies that are exploiting the natural resources of certain countries. Oil, gas, minerals, gold, copper, bauxite, whatever. They do it over in Aussie. They're just raping the land. Exploiting the land. So what I did between jobs was something totally different.

T was on different wages throughout his time in Iraq and eventually decided he'd had enough.

> I started off on £250 a day because of the contract we were on. That went up to £275. Then switched to another contract which was US$550 worked that contract for a little while, back to £250 a day and then got up to £300 a day or £330. Then switched companies and got £400 a day. Normally it'd be six weeks on two weeks off, but one time I stayed for a four-month stint. Yeah, four months solid. And as my changeover date got closer I checked my bank account and found I had a lot of money saved and I thought to myself oh I don't really want to work here anymore. So changeover day came and me and the team drove down to the area of no-man's-land between Kuwait and Iraq and I saw my back-to-back [replacement] and as I got out of my car and into his I said, 'Hey WR, tell the boss I ain't coming back, I'm going home.' And that's when I finished.

T found that it was easiest to keep it simple when explaining to people about his kind of work.

> Some people used to ask me about what I did and I'd say, 'Oh, I just drive a car.' 'Yeah, but what did you do?' 'I just drove an armoured taxi; I took people to where they wanted to go and took them back home again. And I look after people.'

But there are lots of things which happen over there which unless you're over in that industry, there's no use talking to you about it because you wouldn't understand the perspective we were viewing things from. Hmm, here's an example. You might be over in Malaysia or Brunei, sitting on top of a large hill, looking down on a lush green jungle canopy and you think to yourself, what a beautiful picture; look how lovely the jungle is, I might go home and tell all my friends to come over here and see this. Now imagine you're walking through that jungle with a pack on, and along the bottom of the large hill it's all swampy and boggy and there's heaps of mosquitoes and leeches. It's fucking hot and you are pissing sweat and there's no fresh water around, and you think to yourself, when I get home I'm gonna punch my mate in the head for telling me this place was beautiful.

Yeah sure, we can describe the physical topography: the desert in the south, the hills and mountains in the north, the heat in summer the cold in winter. Yep, people can understand that, but when you start to talk about how some of the guys acted, describe some of the violence you saw, or the results of suicide bombings, or describe the actions of people you saw under stress, unless you've experienced it, it's difficult to realise what I'm talking about. Or it's difficult to understand why people acted in the manner they did.

One example, this guy and I were talking this one time – just sitting like this having lunch or something. He was talking about a time when he was driving the lead vehicle with a client in it and they were going through Baghdad. There's this one road called Sadoun Street (I think it's pronounced Sadoon); it's in a really, really busy area of Baghdad and if you're driving at normal speed, you can barely get up over 50 kilometres/60 kilometres an hour because of all the traffic and all the people crossing the road willy-nilly.

Anyway, one time they thought they were being followed and as the journey continued they now thought they were being followed by a suicide bomber. That's what was in their minds. And so the PSD leader told him: 'Hey, this guy could be looking to blow us up, put your foot down.' And so my mate increased his speed a little to see what would happen and as he sped up, so did the car behind them. He sped up a little bit again and the car behind them kept up with them and so the PSD leader said: 'That's it, he's on to us, he's trying to catch us.'

I'm guessing now, but maybe the PSD leader thought that because, if you accelerate or speed away from a car behind you, the car will not speed up as well, and in Sadoun Street you couldn't go very fast anyway, but this car came right up behind them so he thought that for whatever reason, this guy was a bomber and he was trying to get the client. Real or not, this was now *their* reality. So my mate really put his foot down and he was saying he didn't care how many people he almost ran over, he didn't care whether he was on the other side of the road, going the wrong way, he was driving for his life. In his mind he was just driving for his life. He said his main focus was to get down this road and get to a particular turn-off that the team leader knew; he didn't care who he put in danger, he was just going for it. And as he was talking to me this was all coming back to him sitting there. He still looked a little shaken, and that incident [had] happened about a couple of weeks ago. 'Mate, I can't do that again,' he said. 'You know, I almost killed women, children, people just walking across the street – for what? For a job?' He said he didn't want to experience that again and he left soon after.

And you know what: the suicide bomber never did detonate himself, even when the 'chasing' vehicle was close to them. *Their* reality was that the vehicle behind them was a suicide bomber. *Another* reality might've been that of a person also driving down Sadoun Street, trying to wiggle their way through traffic when up ahead they see a couple of big SUVs pushing their way through at a slightly faster pace than everyone else, and so they try to get closer to the two SUVs as they can see the pedestrians and other cars moving out of the way and now he is making really, really good time down the road.

Yeah, so he left. So when you talk about that I can understand where he was coming from. But he might tell that same story to someone else and they'll say: 'What? You almost killed some women and children?' And he goes: 'Yeah, but I was doing it for my job. I was doing it to save my life, to save the guy next to me, to save the client in the back, the other guy.' So how do you describe that job? That's why you always keep it simple.

END NOTES

1. Singer, *Corporate Warriors*, 2008.
2. Ibid, 92.
3. Ibid, 95.
4. Ibid, 95.
5. Ibid, 97.
6. 'US Contractors in Afghanistan and Iraq,', *The Guardian*, 16 August 2010, accessed 21 December 2014.
7. A. Stranger, M.E Williams, 'Private Military Corporations: Benefits and Costs of Outsourcing Security,' *Yale Journal of International Affairs*, Fall/Winter (2006): 4.
8. A. Fifield, 'Contractors Reap $138bn from Iraq War,' *Financial Times*, 18 March 2013. accessed 9 December 2014, http://www.ft.com/cms/s/0/7f435f04-8c05-11e2-b001-00144feabdc0.html#axzz3eUnOgJVv
9. Ibid.
10. Fifield, 'Contractors reap,' March 2013.
11. Singer, *Corporate Warriors*, 2008, 76.
12. M. Eichler, 'Citizenship and the Contracting out of Military Work: From National Conscription to Globalized Recruitment', *Citizenship Studies* 18, (2014): 7.
13. Ibid.
14. Ibid.
15. Ibid, 8.
16. Blackwell, 'Private Military Companies,' 2006, 50.

17   M. Eichler, 'Citizenship and Contracting,' 2014, 6.
18   J.W. Blackwell, 'Private Military Companies,' 2006, 53.
19   J. Scahill, *Blackwater: The Rise of the World's Most Powerful Mercenary Army* (London: Serpent's Tail, 2007), 202–205.
20   'US Comission on Wartime Contracting in Iraq and Afghanistan,' *Transforming Wartime Contracting: Final Report to Congress,* 2011.
21   Ibid.
22   Feinstein, *The Shadow World*, 2012, 417.
23   Ibid, 419.
24   Ibid, 420.

LAND BASED LOGISTICS

Those dealing with the logistics of moving personnel and equipment are often overlooked when people think about the privatised military industry. While administration and logistics are often in the background, they clearly enable the other elements of companies and the industry to operate.

Logistics is 'the practical art of moving armies and keeping them supplied' and involves a range of services such as the general operations of supplying equipment, clothing, ammunition and construction as well as specific services in the field such as laundry, cooking, transportation, refuelling, vehicle maintenance and security.[1]

Logistics is often described as supporting military operations from three lines in the general area of conflict. The rear logistics (third line) deals with repair workshops and the movement of supplies internationally and is commonly located near a port. Forward logistics (second line) involves a staging area that is also close to major transport routes and facilities. Combat logistics (first line) is located just beyond the fighting zone and is a location that can be shifted quickly.[2]

In some countries logistics has been one of the first services within the military sector to be privatised. This is partly due to the nature of the work, where usually lethal force is not involved and many governments have seen it as more easily privatised to civilian contractors than military functions. Privatisation in this area is also used to free up more resources for combat operations. Former US Secretary of Defense Donald Rumsfeld has described the reallocation of resources from logistics to more front line military activities as 'from the tail to the tooth'.[3]

The logistics provided to the United States military in Iraq and Afghanistan come under the Logistics Civil Augmentation Program (LOGCAP), which was originally initiated in 1992. Halliburton was the first company to win what at that time was a single contract to assist the US military globally.[4] In subsequent years, there was a great deal of controversy about the apparent conflict of interest of Dick Cheney who went to work for Halliburton from the US House of Representatives shortly after the company was awarded the 1992 LOGCAP contract. Subsequently, the LOGCAP was divided amongst a number of companies and since 2007 has been held by three companies in particular: DynCorp International; Kellogg, Brown and Root (KBR); and Flour Intercontinental.[5] The LOGCAP represents a lucrative opportunity for those companies that win the contracts. In 2007 DynCorp International revealed that it expected to 'generate annual gross revenues of [US]$5 billion from the LOGCAP contract for southern Afghanistan'.[6]

In more recent overseas deployments, United States, British, French, Canadian and Australian militaries have all outsourced major parts of their logistics to privatised military firms.[7]

As we explore next, logistics represents the type of work that MM was involved with in Basra, Iraq.

MM (TE ARAWA)

When MM arrived in Iraq she had already had many years of experience in logistics. She had joined the New Zealand Army in 1991 and had worked in many of the offices in Auckland, such as at Arch Hill and Mt Wellington Barracks. She had been in and out of the army over the years to have children and she left completely in the mid-2000s.

In the privatised military industry, recruitment usually occurs 'informally using word of mouth'.[8] However, in 2004 MM registered with a recruitment company in the United Kingdom and applied online for a job with a company in Iraq.

> They'd just won a significant security contract. So for them it was a matter of getting feet on the ground because they had this contract with the US that they had to have so many people in the country and it was about the same time I'd applied online. I'd enrolled with an agency ... And I had

probably been enrolled for about a month. I was quite lucky … We did an interview over the phone and it was pretty much a week later. It was really quick.

MM had applied for release from the army three months earlier. Before any formal briefing, or the reality of going to Iraq had settled in, she was flying to Dubai and on to Amman in Jordan and Baghdad.

Landed in Baghdad … And I'm like, oh my God, it's really hot here. I didn't know anyone, but when I was in Amman, I met a British guy and he had just been employed by the same company as me so we started talking and talked on the plane all the way to Baghdad. We had instructions on how we were going to get picked up and this is what you do and this is what you don't do. But you don't really understand it until you get there.

To MM's shock, no one was at the airport to meet her or her colleague.

We got there in the morning. We sat there for about six hours. We were talking to the Gurkhas who were doing the security. They try and help you out as much as they can, but they have limited resources there too. They were talking to people that didn't work for the same company that we did, and I don't even know how we ended up getting a hold of our contact who was sitting in the Green Zone. We were told you jump on the Rhino … that was a big armoured bus that drove from Baghdad airport to the Green Zone every day. The times don't come out 'til that day for security reasons. So they'd given us timings, but they must have been incorrect.

Oh, it was so funny. I was sitting there, it was hot, we had no water, we had nothing, we had no food and then the Gurkhas were like: 'We could give you *a* bottle of water.' They were limited with their water supply, so that was really nice of them. And I remember sitting there. We'd gone outside and we were sitting upstairs still waiting for the Rhino. Then they said the Rhino was coming downstairs, go downstairs, the Rhino will be at the main door, and it wasn't. Some other guy said, 'Oh well, try upstairs because sometimes it is there.' The Nepalese didn't know what time it was coming either. Anyway, we were sitting upstairs and in the distance I could see this big guy and I was like oh my God, I think I know him. And he kept coming closer, closer and he was a Kiwi. I knew him. A Māori. And he was like, 'What the hell? Holy shit, what are you doing here?' And I'm like, 'Oh my God, H, we're stuck.' Yeah, so it was just nice to see a familiar face. So he sat with us for about an hour waiting for his client; unfortunately he couldn't help us, because he was there to pick up someone else. And he'd given us his number, but we had no phones, we had nothing. Anyway, this security company finally turned up and said, 'Are you from Company A?' And we're like, 'Yeah' and they said, 'Right, you're with us.' So me and this guy jumped into our six-car convoy with an American security company. To this day I don't know who they were. And then we drove out. At the airport there was a sort of double cordon. You've got an inner cordon and an outer cordon and we drove to the outer cordon and, to my surprise, it was the *longest* convoy I'd ever seen. There were military vehicles everywhere and Apache helicopters. I'm like, holy shit.

They'd said this was the most dangerous road in the world. People were dying on there every day – security, private security and military. And [when] we saw the size of the convoy, I realised, this was quite serious stuff. It was just amazing and like every kilometre there were tanks stationed just there. I'd never seen so many army people in one place before. It was a bit of an eye-opener. And then we finally got to the Green Zone and they had guys there meeting us. Surprisingly, there were actually quite a few of us. There was one Māori guy that was there. He'd arrived a couple of weeks before me, I think. A bit older than me. I didn't know him though. He was ex-infantry. He'd actually left the army quite a few years before.

As with many of the other New Zealand personnel, MM was keen to find the other New Zealanders and Māori.

Because I knew most of the Kiwi guys who were working over there all I wanted to do was go and find out where they were and just go and hang with them. It took a couple of days, and then you'd just be walking around and you would bump into them. Some of them I didn't know because I'd spent my whole career in Auckland – it was just the Auckland ones I knew. And there were a lot of them there.

At one stage there was another Māori also working for MM's company who MM had known from Auckland.

How many Kiwis did we have in there? There were actually about fifteen Kiwis in the Basra area, including at the Shaibah Log Base or Basra Palace working for other companies. Most of them were Māori or [Pacific] Islander actually. There weren't many Pākehā ... we used to play touch [rugby] ... on the British football fields. Sand. So at least once a week we'd get together and play touch. And we caught up with each other, after work mostly.

Before MM began her duties proper she completed an induction course with her company.

We did our induction there and we were told, 'if you don't pass, we're sending you home.' And I was like I didn't come *all* the way here to fail. I was pretty nervous and really worried. There were a lot of us because that was the first induction course they'd run, but they'd been bringing people in for the last four to eight weeks. So I think there were about sixty of us that had to go through the training. It was their very first training so we were sort of like the guinea pigs. It was over a week, and a lot of it was just firing weapons – AK-47s. I'd *never* used one before in my life – I'd never even carried one. And they threw us on the range ... with those and I was like, what?!

It was a lot heavier and it's got a bit more grunt than the ones we use here. But I passed OK. I don't know how I passed it, but I did. It was all about how many holes you could shoot in the target – not actually how you pull the weapon apart or clean it. Thank God, because I would have failed. So my shooting was fine – it was the handling of the weapon that I wasn't very good at. But hey, I didn't care, I didn't fail. And the pistol – they use the Glock and I'd only used a P226 [automatic pistol], which is a bit heavier. Loved the Glock. It was so much more of a woman's pistol. Loved it. And passed it (the shoot). Not many passed. Phew.

> I did a two-year stint with the same company. And I only came home because my husband decided he wanted to go and work overseas too. So for about a month we were both in Iraq. And I came home. I probably would have stayed there a few more years if my husband didn't decide to go over there.

During her two years working in Iraq, MM had ninety days leave and three free trips home each year to take as she saw fit. She made four or five trips home each year. MM was paid around US$100,000 per year that came in to a New Zealand bank account. As she had children at home in New Zealand it made sense to keep a New Zealand bank account rather than basing herself offshore for tax purposes.

> I didn't want to upset the kids' school and activities by making them come to me, but you know, we could have met in Aussie, or Singapore. I think if I'd known a bit more about that before I went over, we probably could have planned it better. But I'm not going to spend twelve months away from home and probably wouldn't have seen the kids that much. So I'm going to stay a New Zealand resident and I'm going to pay the tax. We had an accountant, so we used him to do my taxes. He probably could have done it better. He did suggest you can start your own company, but he didn't sort of push us to that, so we just paid normal tax, provisional tax and stuff like that and it was a real killer. It was hard. We'd never done it before and we struggled paying provisional tax.

MM found her working conditions suitable given the context and location.

> We were quite lucky where we were. I was posted in southern Iraq, in Basra, where the British were. Most of the other regional centres were American-based, with the American military. When we first got there we were living with the British in their military accommodation. They were like twenty-man tents and the toilets were pretty good, the ablutions – the showers and stuff like that. The meals were great. They had a mess and the Brits were awesome. We were fed pretty well. But we were civilians, so there was still a bit of a thing between the military and private security. I think it was because they were doing the same thing, but getting

paid way less. A lot of them actually got employed while they were there – by other companies, not just the one I was working for. For example, they'd go home after their tour and then the company would just bring them back in. We were in there for about a couple of months until they had sorted proper accommodation.

There was only one other young woman working for MM's company but for her this imbalance in numbers of men and women was simply a continuation of her life in the military.

Well, see, we were living amongst the British military so there were a lot of females there, but a lot more men. I think coming from the New Zealand Army, it wasn't a big thing – it was the norm because it's like that here. So that didn't really bother me.

I don't think there were any Māori women in Iraq when I was there. You start to hear about all the different people over there and who's in, and I think that there was another Kiwi woman when I was there, but I think she was in Kuwait. She was an ex-military person, she was logistics too. I'd heard she was working from Kuwait and I never ran into her, but then I did meet a Kiwi who was an accountant for the company in the head office and they sent her to Iraq. She came in about a year after I got there. I don't think there were many Kiwi women in there at all. Maybe three of us, I'm just guessing, for that two-year period.

The company MM worked for had a contract with the US State Department, which meant she was entitled to carry an identity card that provided her with particular privileges.

When we first arrived we were issued with US defense cards. Because we were contracted by the US State Department, all their contractors had the Department of Defense card, they call them DoD cards. We were quite lucky. At the time I didn't realise how lucky we were, until a year later when they issued us with a different card. We also had to have an Iraq weapons card – it was all written in Iraqi, I didn't even know what it said – basically giving us permission to carry weapons. And that was it.

In 2005, New Zealanders had their identity and security privileges removed and the media speculated whether the cause was the New Zealand Government's reluctance to commit troops to the Iraq invasion. New Zealanders were issued with 'multinational identity cards – which were colour-coded, depending on whether the recipient's country supported the war effort'.[9] The Labour government of the day reiterated its view that 'Kiwis should not be in Iraq and that those who go should expect little help if in trouble'.[10]

MM felt that there were mainly benefits, but also some challenges to being in the privatised military industry compared to the New Zealand Army.

> So I worked in the operations cell and we had an operations manager and we had a regional manager. There was logistics, intelligence, admin all working in the same office., But it wasn't the same as in the army ... I think as long as we did our job, they were happy ... So we did have a structure ...

> You know, you're doing this similar job without that hierarchical aspect you get in the New Zealand military. So even though everyone there was ex-military, it wasn't like that. It didn't have that hierarchical aspect – which works well in the army, but in this job there was a lot more freedom. You didn't get punished for doing something wrong.

> Well, I don't know whether that was a good thing though, because some of the guys would say, 'I'm not doing that.' 'Well, actually it's part of your job.' 'No.' And we couldn't do anything.

MM found that on occasion people, her included, had difficulties with receiving their pay in a timely fashion and much of this involved the banks and their processes.

> It was because you needed a swift code, a couple of codes ... But then I also heard that the banks used to hold onto it for interest purposes. So we'd get paid fortnightly – I remember once I didn't get paid for like a month. My company had done their bit, it was the bank ... So I rang the bank and they were like, 'Oh yeah, I can see the payment.' And I said, 'Well, how come I can't see it?' And they said, 'Oh well, we'll release it in a couple of days.'

Unlike many of the other personnel in Iraq, MM registered her presence with the New Zealand Consulate in Kuwait.

> I registered with Kuwait. They were the closest. And they were cool. He used to send me emails, they used to have like a – I think it was like a monthly update and he'd send that out to all the expats. And we had an election while I was over there – 2005. But it's not like I could jump in the car and drive to Kuwait so I didn't vote then.

Even though MM spent plenty of time with other Māori they never really discussed specific Māori issues or politics from home.

> When I was in the military we weren't that *Māori* back then in the nineties. I think it's only recently – the kapa haka was just starting up when I was leaving the military. We never did that stuff. I'd come home to tangi while I was in Auckland and do stuff like that, but that was it. When I went back to Auckland we hardly talked about being Māori or what we did in our iwi and hapū. Does that make me a bad Māori?

Once MM returned home to New Zealand she found herself getting involved in more local issues.

> I think working in those sorts of places always led you to think we're so lucky back home. I think what it did do was bring me closer to my iwi ... But that's just me. So I do more stuff now than I used to. I was working for a local Māori land trust. I got into environmental stuff and that was basically my first real job when I returned from the Middle East. I think it is because financially I didn't have to work since I've been home, so I've got more time to give to the hapū and iwi. And that's what I've been doing.

END NOTES

1. Singer, *Corporate Warriors*, 2008, 144.
2. J. Seed, 'Privatising the Hard Part: the New Zealand Experience of Employing Contractors to Deliver Military Logistic Support,' unpublished MA thesis, Victoria University of Wellington, 2014, 32-34.

3. D. Rumsfeld, quoted in Seed, 'Privatising the Hard Part,' 2014, 13.
4. P. Chatterjee, *Iraq, Inc. A Profitable Occupation* (New York: Seven Stories Press, 2004), 41.
5. Seed, 'Privatising the Hard Part,'2014, 48.
6. M.G. Haynes, 'LOGCAP Demystified: A Primer on LOGCAP Services,', *Army Sustainment: Professional Bulletin of United States Army Sustainment* 43, no. 6 (November/December 2011).
7. Singer, *Corporate Warriors*, 2008, 98.
8. Blackwell, 'Private Military Companies,' 2006, 46.
9. H. Dewes, 'Kiwis in Iraq Cut Adrift,' *Dominion Post*, 23 July, 2005, 1.
10. Ibid.

MARITIME SECURITY

While T and MM worked solely on land-based operations, the Silver Surfer has mainly worked in maritime security. Maritime security is commonly defined as including 'those measures employed by owners, operators and administrators of vessel, port facilities, offshore installations, and other marine organizations or establishments to protect against seizure, sabotage, piracy, pilferage, annoyance or surprise'.[1] Some companies have their own vessels that travel alongside others they may be protecting but many other companies simply provide the personnel to act as security (armed or unarmed) on vessels until they reach their destination. There are many other kinds of activities at sea which add to the complexity of maritime security. Some of these activities involve guarding stationary oil rigs, assisting research vessels mapping the sea floor, or communications companies that are laying telecommunication cables on the sea floor.

The monitoring of maritime areas and the provision of maritime security has traditionally been a role for state-based navies. However, like the increase of privatised military activities on land, maritime security has also been increasingly privatised.[2] The United Nations Convention on the Oceans and Law of the Sea generally governs activities on the high seas and when vessels enter a particular country's waters they follow the laws and regulations of that country.

There are a number of maritime routes that have long been of huge significance for global trade. The huge quantities of goods that are carried along these routes makes them not only vulnerable when states that adjoin the route are conflict zones but also of huge importance for the companies and countries that rely on that trade to protect the vessels. Particular areas and routes are considered most important and these include the Gulf of Aden and the Malacca Straits that can see, for example, annually around 50,000 ships passing through.[3]

The marketplace of land-based security is increasingly becoming crowded as larger companies dominate contracts in Iraq and Afghanistan that are being tendered out, particularly by the United States Government, and smaller companies are unable to compete. With many of the contracts coming from the US Government, there are specific providers that continue to be favoured, such as KBR for example.

Maritime security is an area where smaller companies have been able to win contracts because the majority of those offering contracts are private companies from a range of countries. Envoy360, based in Dubai, is a New Zealand company which has managed to flourish in such an environment. It has employed many Māori, including the Silver Surfer who worked for the company after a number of years in the industry.

SILVER SURFER (NGĀTI POROU)

The Silver Surfer served in both the New Zealand Army and the Royal New Zealand Navy before moving to the privatised military industry.

> I was in the infantry for two years as a rifleman and then I service-changed because I wanted to do more travel, over to the navy – the Royal New Zealand Navy, I was in communications and I was there for six and a half years. And then after that I thought, I want a bit of a change. My boss actually, when we were in Afghanistan, when I was in the navy, he got me into private security –, kind of, you know, like thinking about it. He said you know, if you want to come along (because he was already out by that stage) then yeah, give it a go.

As with many other personnel who move from the military to the privatised military industry money was certainly an attraction for the Silver Surfer.

> The main drawcard for me at the start was money. At the start, I'll be honest, it was the money. But also it was still kind of military but not

military, you're still working with people from like-minded. You know, you don't have all the rank structure so much – the command structure there – so it's quite cool, because you're more independent. Definitely a lot more independent.

When he started out the Silver Surfer was paid around US$400 to $500 per day. He found that wages varied by company and by contract. He saw some people getting US$300 to $400 per day and others getting US$800 per day. Like many other Māori personnel based in New Zealand, the Silver Surfer's wages came in to a New Zealand bank account and he paid New Zealand tax annually. He began as an operator but in a couple of years had moved to a position of team leader in charge of operations.

The Silver Surfer's first job was in 2009. He'd left the New Zealand Defence Force in 2008 and was in Wellington working for a local security firm, when he got a call from a director within Hart Security who asked him to come and do a job.

And so I was keen as and got my flight details and flew from Wellington to Auckland (we always fly with Emirates). I was real excited and all that kind of thing. And then met the rest of the team there because that's where other Kiwis were flying out. There was one Māori, one from Rarotonga, one from Samoa and a Kiwi. So only two of us Māori on this job. We all flew from Auckland to Aussie and Aussie to Dubai. It was cool. Then waited around for a couple hours then flew from Dubai to Yemen – Sana'a, the capital. So that was cool. It was good once we got there- a new experience for me. Yemen is pretty dodgy. Back then it wasn't as bad as it is now. It was a lot safer. And then our driver came and picked us up, he was just a local guy and he worked for Hart. So he picked us up and took us from Sana'a at about 200 kilometres an hour; they drive real crazy, eh. The main roads are not too bad in Yemen, in Sana'a, but a lot of them have potholes and he was driving real fast. We were all hanging on going, 'What the heck?' Apart from J because he'd worked in Iraq and so was used to the driving. It took us about half an hour to get to the compound. This is the first compound. In the two years I was working for Hart they had another compound after that. The first compound got compromised … So we got to the compound and there were about twelve other Kiwis there. They were all waiting to go on other jobs. So there's probably about eighteen of us there all in the compound. And it was real cool. I didn't know most of the guys because they were all pretty much older. I was the youngest there by about eight years. So … but it was good to meet them. A bit nerve-wracking you know, all these ex-group [SAS] guys and stuff, but it was good and they made me feel comfortable.

I was pretty much at the villa, on the compound, for three days before I went out for our job so I got to look around Sana'a and see what it was like, walk around. It's actually just a real nice city. I won't go off too much but Yemen is the oldest Muslim country by far. Yeah, it is. I would do more tourism there if it was safer. We could only really go out for a couple of hours and then come back. We would go different routes. We would walk one way then go the other way and change it all up. So if something happened we'd have a plan to get back – but nothing did, people were pretty cool. Yeah, so pretty awestruck by the place. Pretty different from like United Arab Emirates and stuff – traditional. It's actually the original.

On the last day there we had our briefings – in-country briefings, briefings for the job, all that kind of thing. Real exciting. Because I was just an operator the team leader said: 'OK, can you get all the kit ready?' So I got all the kit ready and that was cool. Did everything, make sure it's all there and just muster it and all that kind of stuff. Yeah and after that, the next day we're ready to rock. We were supposed to fly down but because the flights are pretty random in Yemen, like sometimes they fly and sometimes they don't, it's really hard to get flights. So we actually drove down. At 200 kilometres per hour. Real dangerous. I think there are 200 accidents a week in Yemen – yeah, it's real bad. But our driver being a local knew his stuff. Overtaking on corners. Yeah, so I think in some ways that part of it was more dangerous than the actual proper job. But good fun anyway.

Yeah, it takes awhile, I think it's about a five-hour drive from Sana'a. So it's a bit of a drive. Then we got to Nishtun. It's entirely a fishing village. The people were sweet as – weren't even looking at us too much, or anything. And then we had our ship there waiting for us.

Some of the Silver Surfer's colleagues boarded a tugboat hired as an escort vessel and the others, including the Silver Surfer, went on board the client ship.

It was a Chinese survey vessel ... it was real cool. Say again. They were a survey ship but this time they were laying undersea cable. It was for the internet cable they were laying for Africa. So we were going at a real slow speed and so then we got taken out from the fishing village and then the tugboat kind of followed us out to escort and that's where the job started. So where was our destination? Yeah, down the coast of Africa, East Africa. Yeah, we had to go past there [Somalia] at a real slow speed so that's why we had the escort – we were only going like 4 knots.

The job was twenty-something days. Without incident. Yeah, we didn't even see any pirates. So that was cool. But we did a lot of training on that one. Heaps and heaps of training so it was good. Because our team leader, he was ex-group and actually our 2IC [second in command], he was too. So we had a real good team. A lot of experience and then us newbies. Yeah, they taught us lots. Every day we were training. Hammered us – but it was for the good. So we just cruised down the coast then cruised back to Nishtun that's where we disembarked, twenty-something days later. Twenty-three days the job, so it wasn't that long. Because you know, we laid the cable on the way down and then we just sped, well – 'sped' back at about 12 knots back to Nishtun. So that was cool and yeah, no incidents on that but jumped off in Nishtun then got picked up and drove back to Sana'a.

We stayed in a hotel– in Nishtun – on the way back but we weren't even allowed to leave the hotel. Because it's a dodgy area. Nishtun, the fishing village, is all right but the actual area – you'll laugh at this, I think, or kind of, the name of the town nearest is called Al Ghaydah [phonetically Al Qaeda]. Yeah, it is. That's the name. So we're staying in this place and it's known for lots of them [Al Qaeda] there. So we're staying in this hotel and not allowed to go anywhere. Didn't want to go anywhere, anyway. Just wanted to go to sleep then get out of there. But that was the name- funnily enough. But yeah, stayed there then went back to Sana'a which was cool. Got our debrief. So that was the first job.

After I got back to the compound there were even more guys there – about seventeen plus our team so there were about twenty-something of us there. Wasn't enough beds. I had to sleep down the bottom. All the team leaders got the beds. But that's cool. It was comfortable. All the villas have marble floors and the mattresses are all good. But the power goes out heaps in Yemen, so you're working away on your computer and it shuts down, eh. But that's the nature of the place. So that's the first job.

One of the ways that some companies appear to diversify their business is by also offering training courses. Some of those same companies strongly encourage or require their operators to take those courses. The Silver Surfer had this kind of experience directly after his first job.

After that, it's real unusual – like I hadn't done any courses, ISPS [International Port and Ship Security Code] course or anything like that. And one of the managers said it's a requirement now for everyone to do the course before they can work again. So I was like, 'sweet as' ... So we went with Hart to Singapore. I could have done it in Auckland but it was good to do it in Singapore. So I got an offer to fly me just straight to Singapore, through the company, and then back home after that. But my uncle passed away while on that job. So that was sad. So if I returned to New Zealand it meant I had four days before the course started. So I flew back to New Zealand for the four days. They'd already had the tangi and all that so that was stink as but yeah. I just wanted to go and see Mum and my sister and they were all good. Then after that I flew back to Auckland and then to Singapore on Brunei Airlines. Which was nice, nice airline. Stopped in Brunei, had a look around there on a tour. It was all right. Not bad. And then went to Singapore for the course.

There were forty of us on there so he definitely made his money, eh. Forty of us at $2,000 each, depending what part of the course you did – I did everything which was $2,500. So yeah, he made a bit of money. But fair enough. That's in a week. Just one week. But he had to pay his instructors. The instructors were ex-army and ex-navy, it was really good to see them. But it was a good course. And a week in Singapore. I think a lot of guys just partied more than actually studied. I didn't. I actually studied on that. Nah, it's good. And then after that I flew back to New Zealand and then my next job wasn't until a bit later, about a month, still 2009.

So that course was in August, September and my next job wasn't until October.

They said, 'You've got the job, I'll call you back in October.' And it was on a ship called the *Niwa*, which was another survey ship funnily enough. The manager's brother was the team leader on this. So he was the team leader and he's real funny, eh. And the manager's son was on it and another guy who was on the first job with me was on it too. There were nine of us on there.

That job was short, only ten days around to the Gulf of Aden. The only thing I can say about that – pretty interesting. It started off armed and then we were told we might need to get rid of the arms halfway through the job. We all got asked individually – who wants to stay on and who wants to get off? Some guys don't want to work unarmed. You know, which is fair enough. And then we all came to a consensus that we'd stay on and then we ended up keeping the weapons, so it was a big thing over nothing. One thing was we had the Yemen Coast Guard with us on these jobs. The thing is, they're armed, we just use their weapons. So we just train them to fit in with our procedures not their own.

But the reason was because we jumped on in Oman in Salalah so the Yemen Coast Guards can't come there of course - so we went down the coast of Oman and then to where we were meant to pick up the weapons but something happened. I'm not sure what, but there was a possibility that they might not be able to get on. That's why they asked us, 'If they can't get on do you guys want to carry on?' But they came on, so that was good. It was lucky and then we went through ten days, no worries and ended up in the Red Sea part. We ended there. And then went back to Sana'a. Second job – awesome! I guess there's a bit of excitement with that kind of stuff. Now it's a bit different, and has tapered off a bit.

The Silver Surfer found that the role of team leader required negotiating a complex dynamic where the personnel are armed but he, as the team leader, is not.

With the Kenyan Government they had their own weapons and stuff and we're not allowed to touch them ... We're not actually allowed to touch them at all. They're the ones that hold them, not us, we're just do the advising, security advising ... they're armed and we're unarmed and that's fine but if it was a job that was unarmed, then all of us, I don't think I'd even take it, to be honest. Sometimes I've heard of jobs that have been paid quite high, but unarmed; I don't think it's really a good thing these days ... Actually, on this contract I'm the team leader and I've got to tell them what to do without them getting angry, like that kind of thing, so you've always got to keep on their side, otherwise you know. I don't know, there's maybe one or two guys I work with who I've thought may not be so right; you've just got to watch out for them, you know, they don't like us because we're there. They'd prefer to have the contract to themselves .... On this particular contract there's a team leader and a 2IC and they're expats and six marines which are the arms guys, per ship but I think one of the ships has got eight marines.

In between some of his Hart work the Silver Surfer did a job for a related company called Vessel Offshore Management.

Well, it was a funny one because the maritime security director at Hart had started his own company, Vessel Offshore Management. And bought the ship over in Germany and so we flew over to Germany. We were there for six weeks getting it ready. It was really cool, got to look around Germany. A lot of it was work. It's a lot of work getting the ship ready:

make sure it gets all its certificates for sailing, make sure it's all registered and checked out, and Germans are pretty strict you know. Well, they had to follow international standards, the international maritime organisation standards. So I was working on there for three months. We went from Germany – once we sailed – we sailed from there down to France, the top of France; it was too rough to cross the Atlantic it [the boat] was only 39 metres long but it's aluminium so it doesn't take a rough sea well. So it was pretty freaky. We stayed in Cherbourg for three days and then we crossed the Bay of Biscay. You have France here jutting out like that and you have Portugal down the bottom. Well, that just gets extremely rough that bay. But it's better than crossing the Atlantic. But it got real rough so we had to anchor in Portugal and we stayed there for a couple of days, then the Portuguese authorities were like, 'OK, the weather's fining up now so you guys have to go.' But obviously it's a haven; we were allowed to go there but we weren't allowed to go ashore and that.

Funny story. Our captain was a bit of a cowboy. Indonesian guy. And he was speeding out from Portugal to go down the coast and turn into the Gibraltar Strait, the small gap by Gibraltar into the Mediterranean and he stayed too close to the coast. It's only yachts and that that can stay there (inshore traffic) and we're like out-shore traffic and he stayed in there, I don't know what he thought he was doing. And I said, 'Hey, Cap, I think you're supposed to go out to the traffic zone, you're in the wrong one.' 'No, it's OK, it's OK.' They called up on the radio and said, 'You're breaching international law, can you push out – this is your final warning.' The Cap goes, 'I'm not doing it we're nearly there.' I said, 'You're going to get in trouble, they've got big radars and stuff, it's not like they can't see us speeding along.' And then I went down and told the ship's manager, a guy called Wayne, he was also in the navy. He wasn't the captain, he was just running the overall management of the trip. And I went down and said, 'Look Mate, he's in the inshore lane and he's supposed to be in the out.' By the time he made it to the bridge, they'd already called up and said it was too late. Well, not too late but you've now been fined. I don't know what happened there, probably got the fine. The owner wasn't happy at all. But anyway, that was quite funny in a way. I said, 'Told you, Captain.'

Yeah, but we got to Gibraltar, stayed there a couple of days, which was nice and then from Gibraltar we sailed through the Med. That was beautiful. We were speeding through most of the way about 29 knots – everyone was trying to enjoy the Med and here was this patrol ship speeding through, oh man. With that captain – the same captain. Funny as. It was only a bit of wake. And so after that we headed to the Suez Canal at the top of Egypt. We didn't get to go ashore but we had to stop in Egypt. It's real funny because all the ships that go through the Suez Canal, I don't know if it's a certain size but you have to let people on board, like customs and small business people; they sell trinkets and things so they have to come on board – you have no choice. So you just make sure they don't go into the cabins because you hear heaps of stories of things getting stolen. But it was cool, they just come on and try and sell you stuff, fake iPhones and things. It's real funny, eh. If you want them to go you have to bribe the police, give them more cartons of cigarettes – that's the way it works. Egypt's pretty interesting. So the more cartons of cigarettes you give to people the less time they'll stay on board. You know, if you don't give them anything you won't get anywhere.

So the thing with that is, every captain of every vessel that goes through the Suez Canal always carries heaps of cartons of cigarettes for the customs and police. And if they don't have cigarettes they give money. That's just how it works. Then you get a pilot on board, an Egyptian pilot, who takes you through the Suez Canal. It's amazing. It's awesome.

Took heaps of photos. Heaps and heaps. You get halfway into the canal and you get to this lake – the Great Bitter Lake – and it's got all these huge ships anchored there while they're going through the canal. Oh my, it's an amazing sight. So we were there for a night and the first pilot comes off and another one comes on for the second leg. Two days in the Suez and you're all going the same speed, in convoy; there's big and small ships just going through, cruising through. We were tiny – this 39-metre with all these huge supertankers and ships. I think even yachts can go through there but I don't know how many do. But it's either go through there or go right around Africa.

At the end we ended up in Mauritius – I got off at Mauritius and the rest of the guys took it to Mombasa. And that's where it is now.

While working at Hart, the Silver Surfer had also done some jobs for a company called Energy and Maritime Security Services (EMSS) whose owner was a close friend of one of the Hart maritime directors. Then in early 2011 he did his first and only job with Barantas, another New Zealand company. Barantas received media attention in New Zealand in 2012 for rescuing hostages allegedly held by pirates off the Somali coast.[4] Despite the positive media attention from that particular contract, other stories began to circulate amongst websites for operators which suggested the company might be experiencing financial difficulties.[5] In November 2013 the company was placed into liquidation.[6] The demise of the company indicates the importance of reputation for PMSCs in order to continue attracting personnel and contracts and the potentially volatile nature of the industry.

I only did one job for Barantas and that was April/May. Start of April 'til the end of May so it was nearly two months. And that one was all over the place. We flew to Sri Lanka, and then from Sri Lanka we went everywhere. Down to Tanzania, Tanzania up to India, India to Pakistan, Pakistan to Bahrain. It was a tanker job so they just cruise around with the oil and then just wait for the highest price. You know – highest buying price – and then they go straight to that port and sell it in that port and they'll pick up some more oil or they'll pick up oil from another port at a low price and then they'll just kind of hang around. That's how it works, eh.

So it was a good job – on a Russian vessel. The food was really good. Yeah, that was two months so it was pretty long. You kind of wanted to get off. Even though the crew was really good, brand new ship, great facilities, it kind of gets a bit boring after a while. The highlight of that job probably was us going to Pakistan. Security never really goes there on ships and the day we got into Karachi, that was the day that the Americans got bin Laden. Yeah, so the day we got into Karachi. Yeah, I know – good timing, eh. So no shore leave. At all. Yeah, it was pretty dangerous. We were doing security in the port. The Pakistanis were doing outside the ship and we were doing it on board the ship – but not with our arms there. If there had been an incident, if we had shot someone or something, we'd be wiped out – there'd be jail for everyone. It was a real thing because we had Pakistani guys coming on and going on and saying to us about how much they hate the States and we said, 'Oh nah, we're from New Zealand.' And then they're like, 'Oh yeah, cool.' I know I've said it before but we've got a really good rep around the world. But yeah, they were really hating on the States [United States] and that. And also the next day there was a bombing at the naval base at Karachi and it killed four Pakistanis and one American engineer. So just shows how dangerous the city is. Very, very dangerous. So we didn't go ashore but I got heaps of photos. So that's cool.

We sailed the next day from Karachi and we went to Bahrain – yeah, that was the last leg. Had about four days in Bahrain so that was cool. It's funny because we stayed at the same hotel I stayed at when I went there when I was in the navy. There's the huge American base in Bahrain and the hotel next to it is the same one I stayed in. Because you want to get off ship, you know when you're in the navy, go onshore. The Ramee Hotel in Bahrain. And it's still the same; I think it's just got more bars and restaurants downstairs now. So that was 2004 I stayed there last and then 2011 I'm back there again.

So that was cool – had a good time. Then we flew back to Dubai, had a night in Dubai and then went back to New Zealand. That was the only job I did with Barantas.

The Silver Surfer took some time out from the industry then began working again in 2012 for Envoy360. He did many jobs with Envoy360 off the east coast of Africa and Oman and looking after a vessel from Kenya to Sri Lanka and to Singapore. In 2014 he worked for two New Zealand-based security companies, Provision and Matrix Security, providing security for Anadarko which was exploring for oil in New Zealand waters. The Silver Surfer did feel conflicted about some of the work in New Zealand given Māori opposition to oil exploration, including by Te Whanau-ā-Apanui and Ngāti Porou.

> I'm not saying I agree with it, but the money is the same as overseas and so it's basically just money for jam, working with Kiwis and that kind of thing. There are quite a few of us [Māori]. It's totally different from working overseas; it's basically just doing security guard work. This is just a fill in. And I did have quite a few job offers to go over for Envoy.

During his time in the industry the Silver Surfer also found himself in some tricky situations that highlight the sometimes complicated connections between the work of PMSCs and other activities such as the arms trade.

> When we were in Yemen and it's a pretty crazy place ... sometimes we had to drive to the port, which is a six-hour drive from Sana'a, which is the capital, to Hodeidah, which is one of the main ports in Yemen. We're pretty much travelling in these four-wheel drives, sometimes with armed guards, sometimes not, and one time we didn't. There's about six police checkpoints on the way – and the one time we didn't we had AK-47s sitting in the back. If we got caught with them we would have gone straight to jail. We didn't have the paperwork for the police with us. So, um, when we got to the police checkpoint – the first one was sweet ... the second one was sweet but the third one they stopped us. They stopped us and they searched the vehicle and we had these AK-47s under all these blankets. They were searching the vehicle and they looked at the blankets and said, 'What's under here?' and we said, 'Oh just our luggage, just our kit.' We had all the papers to get through the checkpoint, from the ministry of interior but ... nowhere does it say that we're supposed to carry weapons. So that was real dodgy, eh. And I was sitting in there and I was starting to sweat a little bit, eh. I was going oh no I really don't want to go to jail here. Especially Yemen. It's just real bad conditions. They looked under but they didn't see. And then they're like 'no worries' and the driver like sped off.

I've done one job where ... we were illegally, actually illegally, escorting these illegal arms. We actually got paid a lot more, heaps more to do it. I didn't want to do the job but just thought oh man, let's just get this over and done with. They were going to their contact ... So we didn't even know the person. And we were illegally transporting them. We got them there. And they got picked up by a skiff by these guys. I'm serious, like just wearing, not a balaclava but a shemagh [headscarf] over their heads. And these got picked up, got offloaded from off the ship and got taken to shore. The captain knew that we were offloading something, but not weapons. It was pretty secretive. ... But that was real dodgy, eh. Good pay, but ... I don't even know why I did the job. Just young.

We got told before we got to the ship. We got told about it and we got told to keep our mouths shut. That sort of thing. I was like, 'Oh my goodness.' Because our job was still to provide security for the ship. Just do our normal job. But not to transport illegal weapons, you know. It's arms smuggling, that's what we were doing. I'm not proud of that. That's pretty much the only shady job I've done.

Off various coasts globally piracy and smuggling are a common occurrence, particularly where countries are subject to a United Nations arms embargo such as Iran, Eritrea, Somalia, Cote d'Ivoire.[7] As the Silver Surfer's experience indicates, operators are often treading a fine line between doing their jobs and being caught up in other illegal activities. It is in these kinds of scenarios too where operators might rely on their management team to protect their interests.

END NOTES

1 B. Deskar, 'Re-thinking the safety of navigation in the Malacca Strait,' in *Maritime Security in Southeast Asia*, eds. K.C. Guan and J.K. Skogan (London: Routledge, 2007), 15.

2 D. Isenberg, 'The Rise of Private Military Security Companies,' *Somalia Report*, 26 May 2012.

3 L. Zamparini, 'Economic Issues in Maritime Transport Security,' in *Maritime Transport Security: Issues, Challenges and National Policies*, eds. K. Bichou, J.S. Szyliowicz, L. Zamparini (Cheltenham:: Edward Elgar, 2014), 43.

4 B. Sabin, 'Hostages Thank Kiwi Team for Pirate Rescue,' *TV3 News*, 27 February 2012.

5 See for example, 'Close Protection World Forum,' http://www.closeprotectionworld.com/maritime-security-forum/81829-barantas-security-group-new-zealand.html, accessed 14 April 2015.

6 N. Smith, 'Bankrupt Kiwi Pirate-Fighters Operating Despite Owing Thousands,' *National Business Review*, 11 August 2014.

7 For a list see 'Stockholm International Peace Research Centre Institute,' accessed 15 January 2015, http://www.sipri.org/databases/embargoes

Boat towing an oil rig

Men at work, maritime security

At work, maritime security

Muscat, Oman

Port Sultan Qaboos, Muscat, Oman

On the boat, maritime security

Swords of Qadisiyah
Courtesy of Jim Gordon.
http://www.flickr.com/photos/jim_gordon/4378390950/sizes/l/in/photostream/. Licensed under CC BY 2.0 via Wikimedia Commons – http://commons.wikimedia.org/wiki/File:Swords_of_qadisiyah.jpg#mediaviewer/File:Swords_of_qadisiyah.jpg

Mombasa

Winding mountain road from Al Mukalla to Aden, Yemen
Courtesy of Shutterstock.

A busy street in Basra
Courtesy of Getty Images

OWNERS AND MANAGERS

As a number of the interviewees have indicated, while the privatised military industry is not as strictly hierarchical as the military, there is still a line of management for reporting. Māori working in management positions, let alone being in ownership roles are extremely rare. In this chapter John and Nigel both explain their experiences in these roles.

JOHN N. (NGĀTI MANAWA)[1]

John is one of very few, possibly the only Māori, to have started his own private military and security company based outside of New Zealand. As a former New Zealand Defence Force (NZDF) member (army), John's life took a different turn because of rugby. In the last three years of John's time in the army he was seconded to coach rugby as part of the NZDF Mutual Aid Programme to Thailand, which involved two or three months per year. It was during the last year tour in Thailand that he was approached by the Singapore Rugby Union (SRU) to take up a position as the director of national coaching to conceptualise, implement and lead their coaching programme. However, four months into his appointment John's employment was terminated. John took legal actions against the SRU and eventually reached an out-of-court agreement some two years later. He stayed in Singapore and went on to work for a Chinese entrepreneur, RW, who John credits for teaching him the harsh realities of owning and running a commercial business.

> I went to work for this entrepreneur in the private club business. We are not talking about nightclubs and entertainment bars but instead, prestigious country private clubs where patrons pay thousands of dollars to become a registered member. They are very common in the US and some parts of

the world and mainly comprise of the affluent in the community. I was the sports and recreation manager.

So now here I am. I've had this successful military career where everything was great and I had a two-year break where I had to try and survive before joining RW at his club. It was two years of trying to get myself back on my feet after the fiasco with the SRU. In hindsight, when I look back it was actually a defining part of my life, it forced me to say hey listen, this rugby was not the path for you. Even though I'd come through the New Zealand rugby system as a provincial NPC senior rugby player and a NZRFU-accredited coach it was not destined for me. People need hard truths in life to tell them where they need to go, this proved to be my life-changing *truth*. So I refocused my energy and went to work for RW.

I vividly remember my very first encounter with RW; I was summoned to his office along with another staff member JR, (the club's professional tennis coach) who was an expat as well. JR was at that time ranked twentieth in the world, so he was a pretty slick player. When we sat down the first thing RW said to us was: 'How are you two going to grow my business?' Right? Being a country boy from Ngāti Manawa, with this army career in my wake, I commenced to waffle on about how I was going to my job. I also explained that I required the relevant resources to accomplish the task, which, of course, meant the financial support from his organisation.

My previous experience handling funds came from the military whereby we operated on an accrual accounting format. This process would require us to submit a wish list before our commanders at the end of an operating financial year for the forthcoming one. So we had this pot of money to use throughout the year so by the time you get to the last day of the working financial year this money would either run out or go below what you asked. It was all about keeping your area of responsibility operating on that budget. At the time I thought I knew everything about running an effective business model; the honest truth is that I didn't understand anything about practically running a business at all.

JR did the same as me and in fact, he was much more laid-back because of our different routes to this point. Living the life of a global tennis pro is much different to that of the disciplined military lifestyle I had. RW pulled off his glasses and said in his Chinese-American slang, 'Mr N and Mr R, you both scare me.' I looked at him and he goes 'Mr N. You're too institutionalised.' I said 'huh?' And he said 'Mr R. You are too casual.' He said 'I want you guys to go away and rewrite everything and compile a comprehensive business plan.' Whoa – a business plan?

I recall doing a business plan at Massey University when I was doing my business diploma. I said, 'He wants a business plan?' We both went away and spent the whole weekend writing this multi-page business plan; it had all the elements in it, logistics, financials, operations, marketing etc ... When we submitted our plans to RW the following Monday, he spent three hours with me and went, 'mmm' and he had this big red pen, you know the dreaded red pen and away he went 'hmm, hmm, hmm' when he finished it I looked at him and he goes, 'Mr N.' and I replied sheepishly 'yes, R.' By the way that was the other thing; I was calling him by his first name R, because I thought being in a developed western community we were free to communicate in an informal manner without all the formalities. Well, he said, 'The name is not R. It is Mr W.' Oops, big culture shock.

I said, 'Oh I'm sorry, Mr W.' He went through the documents and he finally said, 'You have been in the military too long and you are too institutionalised.' Now this guy is very educated and has a few degrees and other tertiary qualifications mounted across his office walls. Initially, I took offence at his terminology and I thought he was telling me I was loony or something. To my surprise what he was actually telling me was that I was too regimented, too institutionalised. He goes on, 'Mr N, this business plan is good if you're working for a large corporate body that has a lot of money but you are here to make me money.' He carried on and said, 'For example, if I gave you $10 on day one, I would expect you to give $10,000 on day thirty-one. Do you understand?' That was business lesson number one in real time for me. I looked at him and I said, 'How the heck am I going to do that?' and he said, 'Ah, now here lies the secret.' He then began to show me.

Within a year, I turned (without a word of a lie) a struggling outlet at his club into a thriving revenue-generating entity. I took on board his comments and implemented them with more focus on effective cost savings, increasing the quality and level of service and creating an environment where total teamwork was the way forward. I was driving those things, which he was really paying me to do anyway. By implementing small changes, like a new marketing plan, and maximising the facilities usage at the club, I was able to grow his business.

RW came to me after the first month of operations and gave me a pat on the shoulder. He showed me last year's P&L [profit and loss], for this same month and I was something like about 30 percent to 40 percent above the budget set by the old manager. Even I was amazed I had accomplished this amount of profit with one outlet under my direct charge. He said to me, 'Mr N you're a fast learner, but don't let it get to your head. Now that you got here, how are you going to sustain it?' Wow. 'You now made that break, you know the concepts and how are you going to sustain it? You're going to plateau out and you may even dip.' And he was absolutely spot on. Children go back to school, parents go back to work, so what are you going to do during that time? So I started looking outside the box at other added value services like early morning ladies walks, early morning swimming lessons for mothers with babies, early morning workouts with businessmen and lunchtime get-togethers with office workers ... and so on.

I went into local schools close to our club and invited them to utilise the facility's down times where they learnt how to swim, (swimming pool) racquet sports coaching, (tennis and squash courts) performed agility/tumble tots gymnastics lessons (indoor gymnasiums) and before you know it I was actually cross-charging other outlets in the club as well because my sales were dining in their F and B [food and beverage] outlets. So they're using my sports and recreation programmes as their business development tools. My contract with RW was for three years and after the first year he said, 'Mr N, you need to move on for both your personal and commercial development.' I said 'No, I'll stay one more year, I need to learn more about the business and its global reach.' So I stayed one more year and at the same time saved funds so I could set up a new training company focusing on swimming, gymnastics and golf for young children.

I opened my new company but only the swimming programme because within six months I had close to 3000 students from six other private clubs in town. I employed local swimming coaches and the business was fantastic, but you know what? ... I had great ideas but I didn't have the knowledge to sustain it on a continuous basis. Then I realised, running my own business you need different types of people within the organisational structure. When you hire an employee, your whole business and your whole life changes. Whether it is one or a thousand people, the dynamics change.

My core business was in the service line. Clients would sign up with the company and the programme because of you. They only wanted you to teach their child but I couldn't split myself up into 3000 pieces. So I was forced to hire other coaches. Some of these coaches were not delivering nor meeting the expectations of service I was previously giving my clients. So many clients started complaining, so I had widened my search globally for better coaches and terminated the services of those local coaches who were not meeting the standard. Later, I realised those sacked coaches were teaming up and stealing my intellectual property and some clients from me. Another valuable lesson in running a business.

So all these points I'm picking up and storing. Then 2003 came around and with it a viral epidemic called SARS [severe acute respiratory syndrome] swept across Singapore. My entire programme just disintegrated from an estimated 3000 students to about thirty. At the same time a good friend of mine, AB a former NZSAS SNCO [senior non-commissioned officer], rang me and said he was coming to Singapore to conduct some training for the Singapore Police Force. Now AB owns and runs a tactical entry exposure school called TEES, in the US. He left New Zealand in 1989 and he's been residing in America ever since. AB and another friend of mine co-wrote a book about their days whilst serving in the NZSAS unit. He came to Singapore and said would I like to get into the private security business because by that time Iraq was in full stride and Afghanistan was heating up. I replied, 'How could I do that?' I didn't want to go over there because I'd been out of the army for a while and my training was outdated. The big emphasis at the time was recruiting former military and law enforcement officers with specific credentials and experience. Later, this became a total farce as many security companies started hiring direct from the streets and as a result, the standard of operating levels fell. AB said to me, 'All you have to do is some revision training.' He continued, 'If you want to, come over to my school and just pay for the transport to get there, you can sleep at home and do the courses for free.' It was another crossroads in my life so I accepted AB's offer and flew across.

I completed AB's tier one courses but in my mind, I said I don't want to be an operator but instead I want to be my own boss. I want to own the company working in this business line but to do this I need to become more conversant and articulate in the subject matter. I required this information so when I submitted proposals and bids I was confident I was saying the right things. I was finally getting what RW had taught me, I was packaging the product in a manner I could serve my customer in order to benefit us simultaneously. Unfortunately, this is an area most Kiwi boys fail in business because they don't know to package their skills and product in the right manner for the market. Areas like legal, insurance, costs, salaries and rates of fees, competition and logistic support. Without knowing it I was building a very formidable base of personal experiences and knowledge through the 'school of hard knocks'.

My partner SP and I discussed the way forward. We had our own tuition classes and were still earning a survivable income and getting through life. We jointly made the decision to move into the security services. I looked at any security be it guard protection or whatever. With me being the only asset of the company – and plus I didn't want to be an operator – I had to be very careful on what route I undertook. I had a lot of opportunities to go work in the sand with the rest of them but I dug deep and held my ground. I knew if I went there I would just become another ant and get swallowed up like the rest of them. Kudos to them, my friends made hundreds of thousands of dollars because of the demand and need scenario in Iraq and Afghanistan. It was mad money; it was like the gold rush times of the past, everyone went over there, guys even resigned from the NZ Defence Force to go over to sell their skills. Even then I could see it was only going to be a short-lived experience for most of them.

So what happened next, I brought all these parts together and then I was introduced to a guy by the name of AD. AD is an Australian forensic accountant. I met him and we sat down, he advised me that he worked for a company called Kroll, an investigative company in Hong Kong and they had just moved into the private military business. Around this time new companies like Blackwater, Triple Canopy, CRG, [Control Risk Group] ERG, [ERG Partners] URG, [Unity Resources Group] whatever 'RG' there is, were opening up and he actually said we should do the same too. So we ended up together.

AD had a shelf company called Background Asia Risk Solutions, BARS; it hadn't done any work, so basically that is where I started. For one whole year I just focused on marketing BARS's image ... we worked for one year with no income, it was extremely tough. Then late one night I got this call from an oil and gas representative and he said, 'our rig has just been attacked, in the Malacca Straits, can you help us?' I replied 'definitely.' It happened about 11:00 o'clock at night when he rang and I was jumping out of my skin. He said, 'First, I want to ask you, have you guys got any experience?' I said, 'I was born for this.' You know, I didn't lie to him; I just didn't answer his specific question. I learnt this method of answering questions from RW and this is why RW is very influential in the business realm, even today. RW is a fantastic business coach and friend. The client asked if I had the experience, I responded 'hey I was born for this'. He said, 'We need you to be there in seventy-two hours.' Can you imagine, seventy-two hours, I have to be on the water in seventy-two hours. I'm not going to go into the details but I managed to get a team on the water in thirty-six hours and moving towards the rig. We boarded the rig with a few other guys, a Kiwi lad amongst them, along with our specialist equipment.

At the completion of the mission and on our return home, I sat down and starting writing the initial templates for our SOPs [standard operating procedures]. This would be an instrumental time – I had to structure and formulate the way I was going to conduct the future operations. The clients were impressed with our response time, the quality of services, shore-based support services and overall conduct of the mission. When we returned home we were inundated with requests for our services from all sorts of oil and gas clients. The marketing had already started and when I got back my partner, AD was smiling, saying that we had twenty jobs already listed down in the order book. I knew then we had cracked this maritime security industry. A quote I remember AD telling me at the time was 'John, this business is like the king of sports: stay on the horse and enjoy the ride.'

I earnestly began to understand in more detail the demographics of the industry and how everything fell into place – every upstream player in the business and then the downstream supporting units. I managed to research in depth what each cell in the whole picture did and how I could integrate my services to grow their business along with mine. I was able to become more fluent and knowledgeable in the oil and gas industry and find gaps in the industry that required my services and this is where I focused all my efforts. For example: how many drilling companies were out there, what types of drilling rigs did they have, who were their supporting agents, how could I assist them to grow their business and so on.

John reconnected with his contacts in New Zealand and began recruiting and employing Māori operators for BARS.

Well actually, the majority were Māori boys but you know, we had some really good Pākehā boys too. The main requisite and criteria for working for me was that you had to be a Kiwi. I actually went back to grab a guy

I'd served in the army with and I also picked guys with leadership qualities and guys that could sit down and write training development packages as I needed to grow my company's intellectual property even more.

My very first team of operators were very expensive as they were former SNCO level and above. Why did I select the group dynamics like that? I also chose a couple of policemen as well. It was to give a balanced outlook to the team: the police guys brought this legal approach to our front-line operations. Our work order just imploded and soon I had fifteen separate teams working on different projects throughout Southeast Asia. So who was in charge of each of these teams? They all came from the first job I did. Of course, with that extra responsibility came extra pay and these guys were lapping it up all the way to the bank.

John began to encounter the difficult job of trying to manage a business successfully to generate profit as well as managing the expectations of employees.

Unbeknown to me, I was actually nurturing competition. Do you see? My Kiwi operators were thinking: why is John getting everything? We're doing all the work. John wouldn't be here if it wasn't for me. You know, in actual fact they could be true in their own mind; this is why I'm saying, this is the ugly side of men and at that time it hurt me personally. These were guys I knew from my military past and even though they were saying it is their strategic knowledge I was using, I would reply 'Guys, I'm paying for that, you are contractors getting paid for the skills and knowledge you have.' They still didn't get it. They believed that my business was there because of them. Unfortunately, these operators did not realise that they were at the end of the commercial link and that all the real work was done before they even sat on the plane to fly across to work.

Generally speaking and from my experience, the Kiwi boys were the worst because the majority are not accustomed to the elements of business philosophy. Compounded with that, you start bringing in Aussies, Americans, and other international operators to the mix and before you know it you've created an international union of workers with many different grievances. AB and I were the only companies offering New Zealanders, apart from the big companies out there, work on the circuit. So the ugly side of big business appeared again. In the end, I persevered and carried on because the work was there and everyone was working for the dollar, which formed a marriage of convenience for all parties.

John found that one of the issues when dealing with personnel was also the attitude towards the work. As Blackwell discovered in his research with PMC managers 'since the primary motives of the contractors is money, there is sometimes an inflexible attitude adopted by them to their work which contributes to their lack of commitment to the overall objectives of the company'.[2] In addition, while personnel are relatively comfortable with a low threat level, once it escalates 'managers often observed reduction in an individual's commitment to the organisation'.[3]

I remained with BARS for another two years and then I decided to move on even though the business was good. I decided that I needed to branch out on my own and take full responsibility for my actions in the commercial world. I left BARS amicably and said my goodbyes to AD. AD taught me the accountancy and contractual side of the business along with proposal-writing. I saw all of that in our business and we did a lot of fantastic work but it was time for me to move on. It was during that time everyone in the maritime industry, I won't say in security, but the maritime security industry, knew who I was. I was one of the major leading pioneers of maritime security at that stage. I officially left BARS; I set up my own company, Maritime Security Specialists, Singapore.

I promised my partner in BARS (AD), that when I left I would start my own bank of clients. Well, that didn't go down very well with my existing client. A few of them contacted me after I left and said, 'Hey John, the reasons why we went with BARS was we can always trust you to deliver what you say.' They said, 'There are only a few John's around the world where we feel comfortable and can count on getting the job done.' They continued, 'We know that if we give it to you, you'll get it done.' ... So some companies left BARS and found out where I was and then they started putting their work towards me.

Around that time, industry people knew I had left BARS. Several major companies from the US and UK quizzed about my present situation but there was one British company in particular that was very interested in talking with me. The company was called Hart Security. I remember saying to them, 'When I was with BARS I was worth one dollar, but now after leaving and starting afresh on my own I could honestly say I am worth about thirty to fifty cents.' I had to be realistic. I went through the entire preliminary interview processes with Hart's management. The chief operating officer at the time wanted me on board but the final approval had to come from the chairman of the company.

The very first time I met the chairman I wore a suit and tie to the meeting, which was at his hotel in Singapore. I pulled up to his room and there he was basking in the sun and wearing a pair of shorts, singlet; he was sitting outside his hotel room, near the pool, smoking this massive Cuban cigar. He was a former British 22 SAS Regiment officer and he built his company around former 22 SAS guys. Can you imagine? Here I am sitting in 34 degrees of wilting Singapore humidity sweating like a bugger and he was lying back all relaxed. This guy is another major learning point in my life. With Hart Security I was able to see the global impact of the maritime security business. His name was SRW. After the formalities and friendly greetings ... he said to me, 'Yes, we know you're worth thirty cents but we want to pay you ten cents for the time being, because we need to see if you can fit into our system and culture.' So I said, 'OK, OK thank you, I'll get back to you.' I hopped into my car and drove down the road and pulled over to the side, ripped off my tie and drew a big long breath and rang him. I said 'Hi, SRW, thank you for seeing me but I'm sorry I have to turn your offer down.'

During the conversation I mentioned: 'Presently Hart Security is out there, BARS as well and now there's one other called Maritime Security Specialists (MSS) run by me.' So I said, 'Now you're going to have to contend with BARS and MSS in the Southeast Asia region.' Hart Security's COO [chief operating officer], called me and I explained to him what had transpired. Suffice to say he was terribly pissed off. As an epilogue to the story for the next four months, MSS successfully conducted something like thirty-odd rig and ship movements, a few of them being Hart's clients and MSS share value rose quite considerably.

John and his partner SP found that starting out in a new business requires perseverance because of the limited income, which initially comes in gradually as the business becomes established.

> We started off in a little flat. SP and I, and don't forget I still had my responsibilities back home in NZ such as home mortgages etcetera ... All that time I was with BARS and starting off on my own it was very hard to survive. We would eat some days and sometimes we wouldn't eat because we didn't have any money. We were truly eating noodles and eggs for meals. I said to SP when I get myself in a solid position, she was not going to work any more but instead just look after me. She had already proven herself to me on what she can do and bring to the business. The other good thing about SP is that she is very frugal with finances but generous in the same breath. Being a devotee and staunch Christian, she would always tithe to our church no matter what the amount we had. Of course, this didn't sit well with me; here we are struggling and she's giving our money away to an invisible person, you know. Unbeknown to me she was praying for me, our business, our health, our protection and general well-being. Until this day, we truly believe that all we have done has been part of God's master plan for us and our generation down the line.
>
> MSS had all this work. And then Hart called me back in June and said, 'Look, OK, we'll give you your thirty cents.' And I replied, 'I'm sorry, now I'm worth $3.50.' Of course, now I've proven myself, right? I wasn't being proud or anything; I had this company and my training department had just been awarded a four-year training contract to which I had just deployed twelve ex-NZSAS guys (mostly Māori). This contract supplemented my maritime security income at the time.

Hart said, 'What? $3.50?' I responded, 'Here's how much I've made in that time.' And they said, 'Holy heck.' I said, 'It could have all been yours but you didn't take it.' They signed me up immediately. I went on to work for Hart from 2006 until December 2012. I held various positions in the company ranging from global director maritime security to director of energy and training. During this time I hired a lot of operators from all over the world but predominantly from NZ and we took Hart Security maritime really global. Even though Hart was global at the time we took them absolutely global in maritime security. Hart Security was one of the first major companies to go through the Gulf of Aden, directly in that area and down through the Indian Ocean. We had set up an operations base out of Yemen.

As a number of commentators have noted, the contracts in Iraq and Afghanistan began to reduce in number once the US troops began to slowly withdraw from Iraq in 2007.

In 2009 I said to Hart, 'We must have a point of difference in our services compared with all the other maritime security companies in the market.' The land work was starting to dry up and a lot of work was moving out. Of course, people started looking towards the water. Hart at the time was doing well. 'These new companies are going to come in and swamp us; we have to differentiate ourselves from them.'

At that time we were chartering trawling and fishing boats to do a security role. I expressed to my management that we go purchase specific boats that do security-related roles. Like former military vessels that can stay at sea for at least a week to ten days and battle various sea states. Not a speedboat, not a slow tug, we want something that can do the job and look professional. Well, at that time Hart was going through a makeshift change in direction in their business model as well. So when I went to SRW, and rightly so, he made a decision to say that was not Hart's focus at that time. This is when I said, 'Do you mind if I purchase the vessels then charter them back to Hart?' SRW agreed, so I purchased two vessels which I still own now. One's a 30-metre US Coast Guard craft and the other a 40-metre ex-German boat. They're presently based in Africa.

In 2012 I made the decision to leave Hart and take a one-year sabbatical to recharge my body and learn how to play golf. My time at Hart was extremely enjoyable and rewarding. I learnt a lot about the global reach of our business and the integration of many service lines in our business profile. Hart was a good paymaster and SRW a knowledgeable man. In contrast many people, including myself (initially), saw only SRW's grumpy business posture but privately the man was a very generous and humble individual.

In the last couple of years I have been dabbling in oil trading. In a simplistic form basically buying it from the source and then selling it to the buyer. Security now forms only a small part of my business profile with vessel management, offshore logistics, medical emergency response and other frontiers occupying my time. I've moved away from dealing with individual operators to a total hands-off approach. I do not confess to be an expert in maritime security or any other form of security-related industry but I can speak confidently on the negatives and positives of working in the industry from an operator and owner's perspective.

When I look back on my life, I can actually compare it to a game of rugby.

Pre-game warm-up: my tertiary days growing up in Ngāti Manawa and living the carefree lifestyle as a normal Maori kid. First half: my military career. It formed the foundation of everything I know today. Half-time: my transition from military to civilian life. Finding a place in the world that my skill sets matched. It was a very scary place to be; you either jumped on the moving train or stayed on the platform and watched everything speed by. Second half: my commercial life. Being a global player in the security industry. Very enriching experiences both highs and lows. After-match function: looking at life's end goal, remaining healthy, spiritually driven and adding value to someone's life through my world experiences.

I know there's a lot more risk, a lot more murky waters and much more rough water to come.

NIGEL (NGĀTI TŪWHARETOA)

Nigel is another rare example of a Māori who has worked extensively in the privatised military industry in managerial roles. Nigel left the New Zealand Army after twenty-two years of service and worked for government in a number of areas, including training, before he began in the privatised military industry.

> When Iraq started up we all heard the stories about recruiting to go into private security. I said, 'I'm into this because the money is good and it's a way of moving forward.' So I ended up heading off to Iraq. I was recruited in New Zealand and then headed off.
>
> I arrived in Iraq in February 2004 and I spent three years there. In the beginning I went there as a trainer. The company I worked for initially trained all the consultants, all the security operators who came into Iraq. And that was a great time for us because we didn't have lecture rooms and we didn't have all those sorts of resources. In photos of Baghdad, you always see photos of Saddam Hussein standing on the podium addressing a crowd and there are these big crossed swords – well that was our training room. We ran all our training sessions at the crossed swords.

In Iraq, Nigel caught up with many of his former colleagues from the New Zealand military.

> You know, that was a big reunion for many of us from the New Zealand military. It was just a big whānau reunion and many of us were in the same teams. I remember one of the teams we had in northern Iraq, Kirkuk, there were five Māori in a team of six and we were all ex-New Zealand military. And you know, the kind of friendship you develop in the forces carries over into the civilian and security industry. Even though you're operating in an entirely different environment, you still trust each other implicitly and it's a fantastic environment to be in when you have people around you like that. And, of course, we were also a lot older and more mature in our thinking. Our tactical thinking and strategising had gone to another level in terms of when we were in the military way back when we were young, so we were able to slip into leadership and command roles relatively quickly.

So that was my Iraq experience and I worked in northern Iraq. We weren't in what they call the Green Zone when we first went into Iraq. The Green Zone was a highly protected area, and eventually we went into the Green Zone, but when we first went into Iraq we actually lived out in Baghdad city, in the city itself, in the south. And we did daily runs in and out around the city, you know, it was very dangerous. And I ended up in southern Iraq, down in Basra, so we did pretty much all through Iraq. And that was a pretty interesting time.

I guess one of the things about the security industry – and you'll often hear people saying these sorts of things – is that there's no security in security. We were constantly working in an environment where we'd come to the end of our nine-week rotation, or whatever rotation we were on, and we would all bring our bags back because there was no way of knowing whether or not we'd have a job in four weeks time.

Nigel was returning to Wellington between jobs but after comments made by the then prime minister, Helen Clark, he decided to base himself out of Australia.

Helen Clark was the prime minister at that time and she made a big statement that all of us 'mercenaries' that were going overseas, to places like Iraq, shouldn't ever get into problems – should we have any problems the government would not support us in any way. That was a statement that really annoyed a lot of guys. And, of course, we were still paying tax in New Zealand and we were paying top dollar. We were earning big money and we were paying top dollar, and the government was taking our money but they weren't prepared to offer us any support should we find ourselves in trouble. That didn't stop us, of course. The money was so good and we continued doing what we were doing. But most people then in the security industry were leaving. For many the thing to do was actually to leave New Zealand, go offshore and not pay tax at all. Many people went non-resident in New Zealand for tax purposes.

I moved to Australia in 2005 and I've stayed there ever since. I'm not a resident of Australia and I'm not a resident of New Zealand. I'm sure I could come back to New Zealand and vote, you know, because I'm still a New Zealand citizen. But what I find is that for eight months of the year I'm out of Australia and out of New Zealand. I'm seldom in New Zealand and I'm seldom in Australia and it's been like that since Iraq.

While he was in Iraq, Nigel found that Māori culture and Māori cultural practices were of great importance to himself and other Māori.

I never had a close incident where I thought geez, that was one of those incidents where you think geez I need to really think about this. I never had any of that. A lot of the guys I worked with did. I had incidents that were not too close but you know, I was in the area when bombs were landing and bullets were starting to fly around, but I never ever once felt endangered in the whole three years I was in Iraq.

And once again because we were Māori, we had this big whānau thing there with karakia, and just having those beliefs and those values and that culture with us overseas, was very, very important to us. Every time we came in, every time we left, we would always get together with the team that were taking over from us, we'd always get together and we'd have a kōrero, a karakia, we'd have our waiata and we'd just finish it off properly. We'd start it off and finish it off properly. That tikanga stayed with us the whole time that we were in Iraq. There were special times when we were often with Americans and we were with British people, you know, and they would think well what the hell are these guys doing? But that never ever stopped us.

I remember one of the first times when a British guy was killed in one of the first incidents with our particular company. He got killed by an explosion. They put a bomb under his car, the car blew up and three people died in the car and one was a member of a team of the company we belonged to. They had his service. And they asked us if we would do the haka for him at the end of it. We were in one of Saddam Hussein's big palaces. They had this service in this palace and I think there were probably at least twenty of us Kiwis in that particular place at that particular time, and so we all got together and practiced our waiata and practiced our haka and we went down and we did it – we farewelled this guy at the end of this service. Of course, people had heard that we were going to do that and some people were, firstly offended and didn't want that to happen, right? And actually left the service when it finished and we were OK with that because we weren't doing it for them, we were doing it for our mate. But when we did the haka, it was that loud and I guess it carried right through the whole palace, we actually had the Americans who were guarding the place, all rushing in to see what was going on and not fully understanding what it was. And when we had finished there were about ten or fifteen fully armed American guards waiting to see what all the noise was.

I think our Māori culture you know, in those sorts of environments, that's when you find it comes out strongest. That connection really, really becomes strong. And a lot of people are whakamā about that sort of stuff, you know. And when they were back in New Zealand weren't particularly strong with the reo, weren't particularly strong with tikanga Māori, but when you brought them in, when they were in that sort of environment, it emerges. There were lots of tauiwi with us as well and, of course, we included everybody – we weren't Māori, we were New Zealanders you know, everybody got pulled into that sort of thing; but I tell you what, our tauiwi were just as impressive as our Māori in doing that stuff. I've found, in general, there is a much bigger focus on our tikanga Māori in that sort of environment. Because you're in a war zone and very often find yourself in life and death situations, and you have to have something, and having something like our tikanga to fall back on is good and a really powerful tool for us. And so I think it's very strong in these situations.

Like T, Nigel found that there was a point when companies in Iraq began to diversify the types of personnel they were employing, away from special forces to other types of peoples and services.

So Iraq was a very interesting time. Lots of Māori there and eventually they opened the doors up to, not just special forces, but they opened it up to guys with military service, guys with police service and we saw more Māori and more New Zealanders come into Iraq. I think probably at the height of it, I don't think I'd be underestimating to say there would have been a hundred plus New Zealanders operating in and around Iraq in that full-on security industry.

Nigel discovered that the balance between the wages he was receiving and the risks of the job tipped and finally became unbalanced.

When we first joined and first went over there, the wage scale was pretty unbelievable, actually. You know, we were earning money that we never ever would have any way of earning in New Zealand and very quickly, probably over a period of three years, that eventually started to drop down and when I finally left, the wage had probably diminished by at least a third. And you really then started questioning, is this job worth that much? Is my life worth what I'm doing now? So what we saw is that most of the guys – from the elite services, most of them – left Iraq and went off looking for other mahi and right up until now there are very few New Zealand special forces people working in Iraq. There are some, but not that many.

Most of the guys left and found other mahi elsewhere. And, of course, that was actually one of the reasons I left Iraq. I thought, three years I've been doing this and I haven't had an incident; the salaries are dropping and the insecurity was still there. I was still packing my bags and coming back to Australia and not knowing whether or not I was going to go back, and all of that gets to you after a while. And so I thought it is time for me to look for something else.

And so I did. I popped off over to Tanzania, got offered a job as a security manager in exploration in the gold mines in Tanzania. The wages were a lot less but at that point in time it wasn't money that I was interested in; I was looking for a change and I was looking to get out of a war zone, and I went into another war zone.

Again, like T, Nigel had found that Māori related to the people of Iraq in ways that other personnel there did not.

Māori are very special people – because we're ethnic New Zealanders, because we have our own culture and we have our own language. What we found in Iraq, it was very easy to get along with the Iraqi people because we could empathise with them. We could relate, we could relate to how they feel. Believe it or not, Māori look a lot like Iraqis. We have a darker skin, but quite often I was stopped and it took me a while to click on to it about why it was that I was continually getting stopped. They thought I was an Iraqi. And a lot of our guys were like that you know. Māori, well New Zealanders, but more so Māori, I've found everywhere I've been, they're more easily able to adapt and fit in with ethnic communities around the world.

Nigel moved from Iraq to Tanzania and then to Kenya and found that being Māori and Māori culture still played a role in engaging with local people. He suggests that one of the ways Māori do this is through language.

I've found that in Tanzania and I've found that in Kenya – because the way to the people is through the reo and we're really good at that. The first thing we'll do when we go there is start learning how to say 'good morning'. You start learning the reo and as soon as you start learning the reo, people change, they change automatically. And even now, my Swahili isn't that great, and not as good as it should be given the time that I've been in East Africa, but I can still kōrero Swahili with the people and it just changes the whole relationship. And you get so much done just by being able to speak their language and understanding. And we understand that and we also empathise with these black people over there because we're ethnic New Zealanders ourselves.

You know, it's funny, the Swahili word for a white man is *mzungu* and, of course, to them I'm also a *mzungu* and I say to them, 'That's the first time I've been called a white man in my whole life.'

Nigel stayed in Tanzania for two and a half years working in the gold-mining sector.

Gold-mining was a whole different security set-up. And I was very lucky, I was in the exploration field, and I set up all the security in our remote camps and related tasks and ran our security and so I was travelling all over Tanzania from the Kenyan border, right across to the Rwandan border, right across to the Mozambique border. And I was running all around Tanzania with myself and my Tanzanian driver. Yeah, it was really nice. You know, I enjoyed that aspect of it.

In Tanzania, Nigel found that there were plenty of Māori working there too and that Māori culture continued to be noticeable and important.

In actual fact, when I was there, the numbers weren't big but we were mostly Māori. We had a couple of tauiwi but I think there were about six Māori, all of us were ex-military, had served together, we knew each other. We knew each other really, really well. Once again, it was like Iraq; going across to Tanzania was going back into the same whānau relationship, you know. We all knew each other. In the New Zealand Army we are a whānau, we are a family, we're Tūmatauenga so, you know, it's all of that. That was a really good time with some really good Māori operators as well.

I really enjoyed that sort of thing. And, of course, once again our tikanga was strong over there.

One individual, he's from Tūwharetoa, actually he was very strong in his tikanga, you know, and he was our kaumatua and so it was karakia and waiata and all that stuff all over again; it was fantastic, actually and it was a good environment to be in. And, of course, we weren't shy to do what we needed to do when we needed to do it. And once again the African people were able to relate to the stuff that we were doing. I remember one day, I can't remember what the occasion was, but at the end of it we sang 'Whakaaria Mai' and as we were singing 'Whakaaria Mai', the whole Swahili group, and there would have been about, I think, fifty of them, joined in 'Whakaaria Mai' in Swahili with us.

And afterwards they came up to kiss us and hug us and we thought wow, this is a great thing and so we ended up learning how to sing 'Whakaaria Mai' in Swahili. And whenever we did anything that was related to them we sang that in Swahili and I tell you what, you want to talk about show-stoppers. It was fantastic and straight away people are just onside with you and you can't do anything wrong. Our ethnicity, the way we were, being Māori, having all that tikanga and everything, that really helped us and a lot of the security things that we did, and I don't know the company ever recognised the value of that. You know, they saw us doing all those sorts of things, but I don't know if they truly recognised that hey, this is really special and we really need to get these people and get more of these people to help us with this. Because it was pretty special when we started doing that sort of thing and getting onside with quite a lot of people.

From Tanzania, Nigel went to work for a maritime security firm, and was largely based out of Southeast Asia. From connections he established in that role Nigel then went to work for an oil and gas company in a project management position. Part of his job involved contracting companies for maritime security off the coast of Kenya. At one stage one of these contracts was awarded to a company based in the Middle East which employed predominantly New Zealanders.

One of the reasons the company won this contract is because of the relationships New Zealanders had built up on previous contracts with the Kenyan Navy. Without the Kenyan Navy you can't do any exploration or any work offshore Kenya, you have to have that connection. So that relationship with the Kenyan Navy is very important to the oil and gas company that I worked for and what happened was, because of New Zealanders and who they are, the guys were able to establish a really good working relationship with the Kenyan marines while they were offshore, you know, they looked after them. They looked after them; they trained them and so, based on the New Zealander content the company they worked for got a very good report from the Kenyan Navy on their performance. So when this drilling contract came up, the oil and gas company said we will only hire Kiwis.

So we brought a lot of those guys that we had in previous years back and the mainstay are the team leaders, so again that whole thing is working really well with the Kenyan Navy... And just so that I can put it in perspective for you, there was another big company which pretty much had secured everything, all the contracts in East Africa, and what happened when we came in was that the Kenyan Navy said: 'We do not want that big company on any of our projects in Kenya again because of the way they treat our navy marines.' ... They were, I won't go so far as to say they were racist, but you don't treat the local nationals the way that they were being treated. So anyway, they kicked them off. And they brought in another company to run that particular project and, of course, that big company really had to go into overdrive to repair that whole image, and eventually they got back. But interestingly enough, the company I worked for were coming into Kenya at the very time that this other company got kicked off that project.

So I came in with the management team to liaise with the Kenyan Navy and interestingly enough, we had to also liaise with the previous company for facilities and assets here. And I remember talking to their security manager and I said, 'We're off over to see the navy tomorrow.' He said, 'Be careful Nigel, you guys need to do this and do this' ... and I said, 'Yeah I think we'll be OK.' And, of course, we went over there and we had the same team and we gave them assurances that it was the same people coming back on – New Zealanders. We gave them the normal blurb that we give them and fantastic, we got a good response from the Kenyan Navy and we got the thumbs up and the green light to proceed. And when I came back, interestingly enough, the guy from the other company rang me and said, 'How did you get on, Nigel?' And I said, 'Great, fantastic, perfect.' And he said, 'What? What did you guys do? What's the difference?' I didn't tell him, but the key difference was the New Zealander element.

One of the challenges and controversial aspects of the management of maritime security relates to the carrying of weapons at sea and which legal regulations govern the use of lethal force in international or state waters.

Any projects done in Kenyan waters, requires the Kenyan Navy to be present. And it's a good thing, really because they actually are the armed component to our project and, of course, if we're talking about law, we're talking about the use of force; we really don't want our guys being involved in any incident that involves shooting pirates. Even if it's in international waters because if our guys are involved in a shooting incident, a fatality, they would end up coming into a Kenyan jail. So it's actually a good safeguard measure that the Kenyan Government have put in place and I actually fully support it.

Typically, on each vessel we have six armed marines and two New Zealand advisors. So the advisors are there to coordinate any response, they will oversee the response, OK? So that if, let's just say for example, the marines get out of control and start blasting off and doing things that don't comply with our use of force rules then our advisors are there to step in and stop that sort of activity, stop that sort of process. They advise. The Kenyan marines provide the muscle and the firepower. So it's a good little system that works well.

Generally, it is actually going that way globally. In West Africa it's a must, and on the whole of the east coast of Africa, Kenya, Tanzania, Mozambique. They utilise the government forces in that scenario. The other thing about having government support like that is access to their assets on the water, so in this case, if the Kenyan Navy are in close proximity to an incident then they will respond, so there are lots of other advantages there. The oil and gas company contract to the Kenyan Ministry of Defence for personnel.

Through his time in Africa Nigel came across large numbers of Māori.

You would be very surprised where our Māori operators turn up. Just thinking right now, on the east coast of Africa I can almost categorically say there are probably 50 percent Māori on our current contract with the company, there's probably about nine down in Tanzania, I know that we have New Zealanders in Tanzania, I think probably max on the east coast of Africa we'd have twenty-five Māori. That's just on set contracts on the east coast of Africa. In the maritime industry we've been talking about so far, those are the operators working on the ships for short term – seven- to fifteen-day contracts, providing security on ships that travel through the

Gulf of Aden and across the Indian Ocean or up to Dubai on the Straits, across the Indian Ocean through to Sri Lanka, or down the Indian Ocean to Durban.

I know even when I was working out of Southeast Asia we had about twenty Māori on the books. I know that other companies also had Māori on the books, you know, so there would easily be, I think, rough estimate forty to fifty Māori people working in the maritime industry, servicing different companies in that industry. And I know on the west coast of Africa there's only one Māori over there. There may be other security related. Because we typically have onshore security companies and we have offshore security companies. And offshore security companies generally relate to maritime security companies. Onshore companies are massive, like gold mines.

In Nigel's experience, he thought most Māori in the industry had offshore accounts although he cautioned that it was difficult to estimate since people kept their finances fairly private.

Most of them deal with offshore accounts and that's because of the tax implications. There was a lot of miscommunication right at the very beginning and there continues to be a lot of miscommunication about tax policy and implications. I do know people in the industry who have been stung really badly and done really poorly out of bad advice on tax. Pretty much set them back, pretty much to square one where they were prior to when they left, you know. There are always those stories.

I still maintain my properties in New Zealand, I still maintain bank accounts in New Zealand and I still file tax returns in New Zealand. Because my aim is always to come back to New Zealand at some point and so I need to keep that side of it all squeaky clean because I can't afford to be caught out when I do come back to New Zealand and having to pay the New Zealand Government oodles and oodles of money in back tax. And so I got really good advice from Inland Revenue, believe it or not.

It was good, actually, all the things I've had to go through and I have to say I'm probably one of the few good luck stories. I guess it's that old wairua coming through again from way back from my mum.

Nigel is currently looking to settle back in New Zealand, somewhere warm.

END NOTES

1 John wishes to dedicate this chapter to his late brother. John told me his brother 'was 47 years old when he passed on in 2011, he had the maritime security industry at his feet having executed over 200 missions on the water'.

2 Blackwell, 'Private Military Companies,' 2006, 53.

3 Ibid, 54.

REFLECTIONS

The aim of this book was to detail some of the experiences of Māori in this industry and in doing so to encourage a reflection on how they fit in the Māori economy. In the preceding pages I outlined the context of the industry and conversations about it as well as the stories of people who have worked and continue to work in it. These stories are complex and contain contradictions. For example, as T explained, he was well aware PMSCs are entwined with the extractive industries and so for him it was important to balance that exploitative aspect with other activities, such as helping to coach rugby in Cambodia between jobs. In addition, a number of the others interviewed did not find their Māori identity particularly relevant while working but do keep close contact with their hapū. One of the insights that can be drawn from these complexities is that definitions of what it means to be Māori and the Māori economy need to be broad enough to acknowledge this diversity.

And this returns me to some of the questions that I posed at the beginning of this book: do current definitions of Māori and the Māori economy enable an account of this diversity? And if not, how else can we frame these Māori and their work so that they are incorporated?

One preliminary question to answer is – why does it matter? Surely there are many random jobs that Māori are involved in that cannot all be accounted for? Surely a definition needs to limit and categorise the most significant of the jobs Māori do? These are fair points. However, what I am suggesting here is not that we need to endlessly add jobs to a definition of what gets included in a Māori economy but rather that if there are a range of activities that though significant, in monetary and non-monetary terms, are not being included, then perhaps a closer examination is needed of how definitions are being formed and what assumptions they are premised upon.

Over the last decade numerous conversations about the 'Māori economy' have begun to emerge. Partially these conversations have been driven by government departments seeking ways to quantify: assets held by Māori individuals, organisations and businesses, and rates of employment, in tandem with the government's Treaty of Waitangi settlements process.[1] In particular, successive governments have sought these quantifications in order to promote a particular type of 'economic growth' to Māori, reflecting government bias towards neo-liberal policies. They have placed a significant emphasis on encouraging 'productivity' (defined as activities contributing to GDP), 'export orientation' and 'assessing 'growth' by also using gross domestic product (GDP) measures.[2]

Discussions about the 'Māori economy' have also been driven by Māori academics, building on research about Māori development and well-being and trying to identify features that may be unique to Māori businesses and commercial enterprises.

There are a number of ways to define the 'Māori economy'. The first key aspect is to look at Māori as employees in any kind of industry. Examining the wages, rates of employment and types of industry Māori people work in gives one layer of what a 'Māori economy' comprises. How Māori articulate themselves as Māori in specific industries is not an area that has been well examined, however.[3]

The second aspect relates to businesses owned and operated by Māori people, again in any kind of industry. Here much of the academic research has looked closely at these businesses to see if there are factors that are common to, and can clearly identify, a 'Māori business'.[4] Chellie Spiller et al. have examined the unique ethical decisions that are made in Māori businesses and argue that these are often related to Māori cultural practices or histories.[5]

The third aspect that is commonly stated as making up the 'Māori economy' is Māori land.[6] Māori land is a specific title of land, as set out in Te Ture Whenua Māori Act/the Māori Land Act 1993. Under this act the kinds of governance entities that can manage Māori land are prescribed and the Māori Land Court has jurisdiction to make decisions, including in situations of disputes about the land. The most common entities that govern Māori land are Ahu Whenua trusts and incorporations. Both of these types of entities have trustees or directors who manage the assets and a particular list of owners to whom they report and to whom dividends or other proceeds are paid or available.

The fourth aspect of the 'Māori economy' involves the assets returned to iwi governance entities as part of the government's treaty settlements process. These settlements of past Crown breaches of Te Tiriti o Waitangi can include both land-based assets (buildings, farms etcetera) as well as money and tend to be managed by asset holding companies established as part of iwi Rūnanga. Asset holding companies all vary in the decisions they make about investments and how they distribute the profits back to the iwi Rūnanga, but are seen as central components of a 'Māori economy'.

These common definitions of the 'Māori economy' are faced with two primary challenges. The first is that despite the range of elements that comprise it, three particular industries receive the majority of attention: 'agriculture, fisheries and forestry'.[7] These three sectors are significant in terms of being the dominant form of business for most Māori land trusts and incorporations and the amounts of money involved. BERL estimates that the Māori asset base in these three industries is NZD$10,579 million.[8] However, this focus marginalises all the entities, assets and transactions that comprise a wider and more diverse economy. For example, these numbers do not include the illegal economy or the markets that do not involve money but instead rely on say barter exchange, koha and gifting. A report in 2007 by the New Zealand Office for the Community and Voluntary Sector found that Māori contribute to a range of voluntary activities, such as the management of marae (traditional meeting houses) and tribal organisations and have proportionally higher rates of volunteering than non-Māori.[9] There is much anecdotal evidence about the significant time Māori connected with tribal organisations commit to participating on governance bodies or with projects related to economic development. Volunteering or working without a salary is often invisible work and part of a hidden economic landscape.[10] Even Treasury New Zealand has noted that what they describe as a 'non-observed economy' of underground production, informal activity, household production and the production and distribution of illegal goods may have averaged approximately 12 percent of GDP from 1999 to 2006.[11] The dominant focus on three particular industries also marginalises significant, but non-dominant clusters of workers. For example, the New Zealand Defence Force is the single largest employer of Māori with 22 percent of all army personnel being Māori.[12]

The second challenge to the way the Māori economy is commonly defined is that only those Māori employees, businesses and assets located in New Zealand are examined. Given one in five Māori live overseas, this really only offers a partial picture of the wealth and well-being and activities of the Māori economy.[13] In addition, statistics from a 2012 Kiwi expats abroad study indicate that 21.5 percent of Māori living overseas in 2012 owned shares in Māori land or a Māori business, which suggests that although they are based overseas they maintain clear economic and cultural links to New Zealand.[14]

Furthermore, Tahu Kukutai's emerging research about Māori in Australia indicates specificities about workers in particular countries. She found that Māori in Australia are 'disproportionately concentrated in lower skilled jobs by comparison with the national Australian workforce'[15] and that those jobs are largely in the mining sector as labourers and machine operators and drivers. Kukutai's research suggests that types of Māori occupations can be country specific. Therefore, making assumptions about a 'Māori economy' based solely on the information about occupation and assets held in one particular country, albeit the 'home' country, might not only be extremely limited but also give a false picture of a Māori economy.

The important overall point is to recognise that the dominant definitions of a 'Māori economy' rely on, and privilege, a particular definition of being Māori. In some ways this situation parallels the debates that feminists have raised about women's work in the home. For many years the work of 'housewives' was not considered 'work' or as important as the waged labour of men – even though as feminists showed, women's work in the home had a social and economic value.[16] Here there are parallels. The privatised military industry has a social and economic value for Māori and the Māori economy.

It is still difficult to exactly quantify the value of the privatised military industry to the Māori economy, because of the limited data about how much money is made and contributed and what non-monetary contributions also take place. As T suggests, I would need to ask each Māori working in the industry individually about their unique circumstances to produce even a rough estimate. In terms of estimating the numbers of people involved, however: from my research I would conclude that a *conservative* number of Māori annually employed in a variety of jobs in land-based and maritime security would be two hundred. My *conservative* estimate of a current average wage would be US$300 per day. Assuming a six-week on and two-week off rotation and excluding those weeks off, a *conservative* estimate of annual wages per person equals US$84,000. Added together those two hundred workers could be bringing US$16,800,000 (approximately NZ$22,396,118) directly or indirectly into New Zealand annually.

Results from the New Zealand 2013 Census in part assist with estimates of Māori involved in the industry. It should be noted that the census takes a 'snapshot' of New Zealand at a particular time, meaning that those workers overseas at the time of the census would not be included. The total number of Māori who stated in the 2013 census that they work in the security or defence sector was 6540.[17] Of that number most are employed by the state, either in the New Zealand Defence Force, Police or Department of Corrections – 4641. This number is still significant given Māori employed in the privatised industry come from these occupations. A significant number of respondents in this category also stated that they were employed in 'investigation and security services' – 1089. In the top ten occupations of Māori in the security or defence sector 732 people said they were 'security officers'. This category includes occupations that are likely to be domestically based (burglary protection, locksmith services) but also others which could be domestic or international (security guards, nightwatchmen, bodyguard services, armoured car services).[18] Some of the people interviewed for this book also stated that they worked as security guards or bouncers within New Zealand between jobs, so there is likely to be a fair amount of overlap.

Table 1

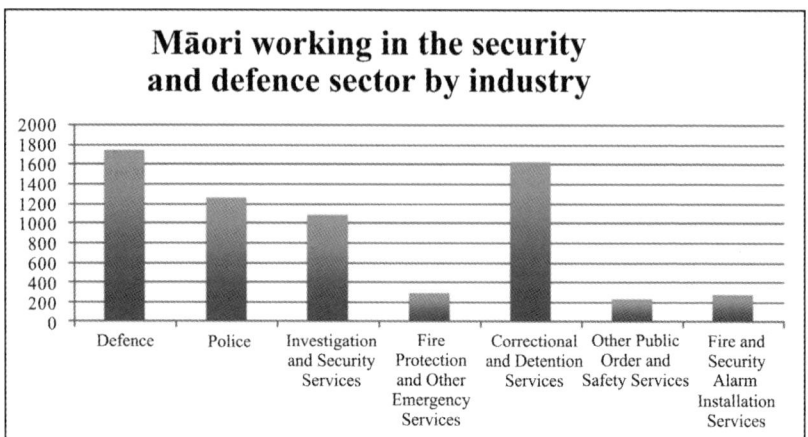

Source: Statistics New Zealand, 2013 Census.

Table 2

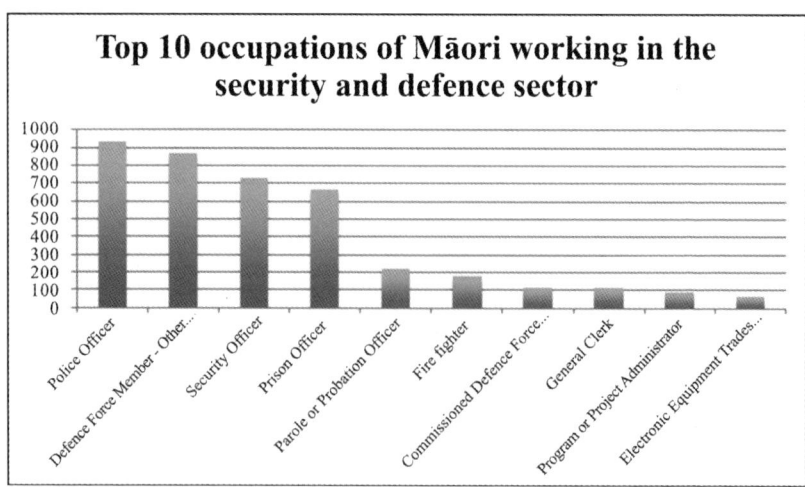

Source: Statistics New Zealand, 2013 Census.

The interviews in this book have indicated that monetary and non-monetary contributions are being made by Māori in the privatised military industry to the Māori economy, including for example through: time and work volunteered for a variety of hapū and iwi projects and money provided to family members for jobs in the industry as well as for tangi, international trips and assets. In Figure 1

Figure 1. Actors and actions in a diverse economy of Māori in the privatised military industry

Labour	Enterprise	Transactions	Property	Finance
Wage	**Capitalist**	**Market**	**Private**	**Mainstream Market**
High wage operators on contracts working for TNCs Salaried managers working for oil companies	Large company operating across the globe HQ in London Small company based in Singapore but with operations off African east coast	Contract for security services with US Department of Defence Contract to large oil company to provide security for oil exploration boats	Intellectual property for security training manuals Boats for maritime security Natural resources owned by states.	Bank finance to buy weapons and other equipment Buying shares in NZ retirement homes Kenyan Government receiving royalties from oil.
Alternative Paid	**Alternative Capitalist**	**Alternative Market**	**Alternative Private**	**Alternative Market**
Self-employed operators taking short-term close protection contracts	Programme management company engaged in sustainable development projects Afghanistan	Buying and selling guns in market Baghdad streets	Armour plates issued from army used for private work	Micro-finance from an urban Māori authority to start a small security company
Unpaid	**Noncapitalist**	**Nonmarket**	**Open Access**	**Nonmarket**
Helping out hapū with resource consent applications Grandmother caring for mokopuna while parents work in Iraq	Hapū Rūnanga in Murupara based on collective decision-making and communal assets	Weapons signed out from a state military while officers take leave Paying for family to travel to Gallipoli commemorations	Security updates from companies online	Loan from a family member to set up a small office Donations to the marae

I have used categories from Gibson-Graham, Cameron and Healy's diverse economy framework to indicate just how interconnected the actors and actions of Māori in the privatised military industry are with their lives in New Zealand.[19] Gibson-Graham, Cameron and Healy argue that a diverse economy framework provides 'a template for a more comprehensive inventory'[20] and highlights people's multiple roles and relationships. People are never only a consumer or a worker or an owner of a company. Instead, people can inhabit all of these multiple roles.[21] The diverse economy is one that recognises and includes a wide range of types of labour, enterprises, transactions, property and finance. The diverse economy framework invites a rethink of how the Māori economy works in a complex and global way. It also reveals the economic activities that might be strengthened and developed in order to further support Māori communities, relationships with other people and the environment.

Figure 1 reinforces comments made by the people I interviewed who saw the contributions of Māori to the Māori community and economy occurring in many direct and indirect ways through their support for their families and their families' support for them.

Although T thought that Māori in the industry might not be specifically contributing in overt and direct ways such as funding iwi initiatives, he did outline many avenues that Māori were contributing to the Māori economy through their relationships with whānau, hapū and iwi. In many respects T's perspective reinforces the importance of viewing these activities as part of a diverse economy and noting peoples' multiple roles and contributions.

> ... so once I got back to New Zealand my priorities centred around whānau. In fact, I would say the majority of my mates who worked over there had the same idea. Sure, the Pākehā Kiwis would say 'family' instead of whānau, but generally I think they had the same idea, and yep, although a lot of us might have said we were there for the money, in the end the money we were making was for our whānau/families whatever that meant for each one.

Is that a large amount of money coming back into the New Zealand economy? It sure is. And yep, so at a purely fiscal level the guys buy flash houses, they set themselves up in business, they set their families up and from my perspective, that's money coming into the New Zealand economy.

As for contributing to the Māori economy, well, I don't know about the *Māori economy*, I know a little about the New Zealand economy and how I contribute to it through my taxes. I know a lot about the economy of my household and how I contribute directly to it through my wages to pay the bills, but how I contribute to the *Māori economy*? Well, that's a little bit different. I know I gave a lot of my money to my sisters to help them purchase their first homes and now as a consequence, they find it easier to support their kids and their cousins …

Hmm … take the New Zealand 'middle class' for instance: for non-Māori/non-Polynesian New Zealanders, being 'middle class' means having more choices for yourself and your immediate family. You may be able to choose what new car to buy, you may be able to choose where you would like to take the family on holiday, what sports your kids can participate in, what school you would like to send your kids to and it seems a little easier to fulfil what *you* consider are your responsibilities. For Māori and Pacific Islanders though, it seems that being in the 'middle class' merely increases your capacity to help others within the wider whānau, hapū, iwi and as a result, your responsibilities increase accordingly.

So after being at home for an extended period of time, I now find myself participating in a lot of marae-based activities. I help row our waka out on the moana and even got to row it on the Waikato. I used to go along to Matatini practices. I attend a variety of hui and I give my time and effort when I can, like go hunting, ruku kaimoana (dive for seafood), help out in the kitchen (shucking the kina and mussels, peeling spuds), help with the hāngi, help with tangi, and yes, still doing the dishes and putting the chairs away and, of course, all of this is done for free.

What the other guys do, I don't know. I do know a couple, or three, of my mates from up Whanganui, they help their whānau and wider whānau out, they organise stuff, like a hunting competition. I think they try to help out their respective local marae up there – they do what they can. As for all the other Māori who worked over in Iraq (and other countries) you'd have to ask them individually how they think they contributed. Maybe it's just the fact that they set good examples, good role models for their tamariki and other kids to follow, maybe it's through the various mahi they undertake that they provide alternate pathways to a positive lifestyle. Who knows really, you're gonna have to do a study on the subject I guess, eh?

I think there is a difference though between people raised as a member of a collective (whānau, hapū, iwi) and people raised as individuals – and this applies to those living in the cities as well as those from rural areas. I now live next to my marae and have cousins who have lived next to the marae all their lives. They have no choice about what they want to do when there is a hui on, whether they want to or not they are over there at the marae balancing their work and other whānau commitments with their commitments to the collective – the marae.

Has the money that I have brought back gone into the Māori economy? I scratch my head a bit when you talk about the 'Māori Economy'. It prompts too many questions for me. What is it exactly? ... All I know is that the money I have earned overseas has gone back into my wider whānau. Therefore, I think the use of the term 'Māori economy' in this instance is a 'red herring'. Perhaps we could use the phrase 'Māori cultural economy' because when we get back home, back to the marae, it's not just the money that is of value, it's the sharing of knowledge, both yours and others, it's the proficiency you have of tikanga/kawa, it's the value of participation in communal activities, it's the value of whakawhanaungatanga, it's the value of seeing others in your whānau doing well, it's the value and pride you have in identifying yourself as part of a larger collective. It's the value of being Māori.

The ways in which Māori are contributing to the diverse Māori economy is also impacted by tax regulations. As a number of those interviewed mentioned, the tax situation in New Zealand led some Māori to base themselves out of other countries, particularly Australia. Although this was to enable them to be a non-resident for tax purposes (for the income received from working in the privatised military industry), most of them continued to pay tax on other assets and income based within New Zealand. The statistics from the 2012 KEA [Kiwi expats abroad] survey indicates that 44 percent of Māori overseas reported having 'financial or formal investment in Māori land or business'[22] so are likely continuing to make monetary contributions – for example, in the form of rates payments on Māori land.

In his research about Māori in Australia in 2007, Paul Hamer found no evidence of an overt culture of Māori in Australia sending remittance payments per se back to family in New Zealand as, for example, many Pacific Islanders in Australia do. However, similar to what I have described here as part of the diverse economy, he noted numerous other connections and ways Maori in Australia were contributing.

... whānau in Australia raising 'at risk' children for their New Zealand kin, or helping New Zealand whānau settle in Australia and find work, or paying board for their own children to return for spells to New Zealand, or even becoming financial members of New Zealand political parties. Many also return to New Zealand to live with increased skills and more savings than when they left. Furthermore, there are many Māori in Australia paying rates on Māori land in New Zealand, not just for the benefit of their whānau but also as investments for themselves for their planned return home.[23]

This culture of 'giving back' to the diverse Māori economy continues with 43 percent of respondents to the 2012 KEA survey indicating that they provide 'support to family or friends in New Zealand, either regularly or on an occasional basis'.[24]

John argues that there is a place for Māori who have had business experience in the privatised military industry to 'give back' and contribute to their iwi by sharing their knowledge in regard to iwi activities.

I happened to be home visiting my elderly mother when a Rūnanga meeting was held at one of the local pā. I escorted my mother to the meeting and I listened to the hui unravel its agenda. As the meeting progressed, I notice two Pākehā gentlemen from Rotorua who were representatives from a financial institute (bank) sitting on the stage next to the committee members. They were passing a motion to allow these bankers to use their (Rūnanga) funds for reinvestment purposes. These gentlemen actually handled the private funding investment of their respective bank. So in essence, these guys would use the Rūnanga's money and find projects they could invest that would hopefully bring a positive fiscal return. They're sitting there and everyone's happy. I'm sitting in my chair remaining silent recollecting to myself I deal with these types of guys every day, then I said John, do you really want to ask this question? Maybe it was a spiritual intervention that told me, 'Yeah, get up.'

So I stood up and I introduced myself. I said, 'Actually my question is for those two gentlemen there.' I asked them, 'What are your expected ROI [return on investment] for the funds invested?' and they looked at me, maybe this Māori boy knows what he's talking about. I said, 'What are the terms of the investment?' Then, 'What's the expected return we can expect after costs?' ... So there's three questions in the one. And, of course, by this time all relatives started looking at me ... But you know what?

I said, 'Stop, hold it, wait,' and I kind of, now my army teachings kicks in and I say, 'I think I need to put a hold on this. Mr Chairman, please. Can I just address the forum?' And I said, 'All you people here are my cousins and unfortunately I haven't been here for the last thirty-five to thirty-six years but I deal with these sorts of men every day.' I said, 'Do you really understand what they're going to be doing with your money?' And then one of my aunties said, 'Yeah, they're going to go make money for us.' And I said, 'Actually, you're quite right, they are. But do you understand the dynamics of how they're going to make that money? Have they presented you a business plan or an investment plan to show you how they're going to make it or where they're going to invest it? Have they shown you what their rates are?' I said, 'One percent per annum or one percent of each deal?' You see things like that. I said, 'Basically what I'm saying is have you done your due diligence?' Then you could hear my uncles saying, 'Yeah, yeah, boy, keep going.' And I said, 'Actually, I'm not here to do that,' and I said, 'listen, I think I need to explain what these gentlemen's roles are.' I explained it to them in layman's terms and you could see my aunties and all my cousins shaking their heads. And then one of my aunties stood up and pointed to these guys and said, 'Now tell us what we can expect?' ... and then they started explaining and then my aunty couldn't understand and she said to me: 'Boy, explain that to us' ... You asked me where can we fit back with our iwi? This is just one of them.

There are opportunities for Māori from the privatised military industry to contribute in novel ways to hapū and iwi. In recent years many iwi have been investigating renewable energy production options. With a proportion of Māori in the privatised military industry trained in engineering, building, demolition and project management, their skills might well be utilised by iwi. This is a track pursued by other indigenous peoples. To give an American example, with high rates of indigenous veterans living in indigenous communities, Native American environmentalist and economist Winona LaDuke has encouraged the involvement of these veterans in building renewable energy structures. For the White Earth Reservation that she belongs to in Minnesota she engaged US Army veteran Tony Tibbetts to build the first wind turbine on the Reservation.[25] LaDuke argues that indigenous communities 'have a lot of people in the military that have a skill set that needs to be reapplied to a peacetime economy'.[26]

What is at stake if the definition of the 'Māori economy' remains narrow and disproportionate attention continues to be paid to specific sectors of Māori in New Zealand? Such a view limits the ability of Māori to adequately plan political and economic governance entities that reflect and represent the diversity of Māori economic situations and activities. A diverse economy's framework illuminates hidden economic activities and ways of being Māori and allows a more nuanced, more inclusive and ultimately, more accurate view. The stories and experiences of people outlined here provide a reminder of this hidden economy and the need for their inclusion.

END NOTES

1 See for example, Te Puni Kōkiri, *He Kai Kei Aku Ringa: The Crown Māori Economic Growth Partnership* (Wellington: Te Puni Kōkiri, 2012); Te Puni Kōkiri, *Māori Demographics for Economic Return* (Wellington: Te Puni Kōkiri, 2011).

2 See for example, Te Puni Kōkiri, *Māori Export Competitiveness* (Wellington: Te Puni Kōkiri, 2011); or Te Puni Kōkiri, *Lifting Māori Productivity* (Wellington: Te Puni Kōkiri, 2010.)

3 One of the few pieces of work to consider this within organisations J. Bryson, P. O'Neil and H. Lomax, 'Developing Human Capability: Employment Institutions, Organisations and Individuals: Māori Research Strand' (Discussion Paper, 2008). And another which looks at Māori women in accountancy, P. McNicholas, M. Humphries, S. Gallhofer, 'Maintaining the Empire: Māori Women's Experiences in the Accountancy Profession,' *Critical Perspectives on Accounting* 5, no. 1 (2004).

4 P. Tapsell, C. Woods, 'Pōtikitanga: Indigenous Entrepreneurship in a Māori Context,' *Journal of Enterprising Communities.*2, no.3, (2008).

5 C. Spiller, et al., 'Relational Well-Being and Wealth: Māori Business and an Ethic of Care,' *Journal of Business Ethics* 98, no.1 (2011).

6 T. Kingi, 'Cultural Bastions, Farm Optimisation, and Tribal Agriculture in Aotearoa New Zealand' (Proceedings of the 22nd International Grasslands Conference, 2013).

7 Te Puni Kōkiri, 'Māori Demographics for Economic Return' (2011).

8 Ministry of Business, Innovation and Employment, 'A Snapshot of the Māori Economy' (2010).

9 Office for the Community and Voluntary Sector, 'Mahi Aroha: Māori perspectives on volunteering and cultural obligations' (Wellington: Office for the Community and Voluntary Sector, 2007), 16.

10 J.K. Gibson-Graham, *A Postcapitalist Politics* (Minneapolis: University of Minnesota Press, 2006).

11 E. Gorman, G. Scobie, Y. Paek, 'Measuring Saving Rates in New Zealand: An Update' (Treasury Working Paper, 2013); see also, A. Bollard and R. Barrow, 'Could we be better off than we think?' (Speech to the Trans-Tasman Business Circle, Auckland 2012).

12 *Te Ara Encyclopedia of New Zealand*, 'Armed Forces', accessed 28 June 2015 http://www.teara.govt.nz/en/graph/35716/defence-force-personnel-by-gender-and-ethnicity-2012. Te Puni Kōkiri put the numbers of Māori in the army at 20% in 2008. (Te Puni Kōkiri, September 2008).

13 Te Puni Kōkiri, *Every Māori Counts*, 2012.

14 Ibid.

15 Kukutai and Pawar, 'A Socio-demographic Profile', June 2013,' 58.

16 M. Waring, *If Women Counted* (San Franscico: Harper & Row, 1988).

17 The total number (Māori and non-Māori) for New Zealand was 41,565.

18 Statistics New Zealand classification codes, accessed 25 January 2015, http://www.stats.govt.nz/tools_and_services/ClassificationCodeFinder/ClassificationCodeHierarchy.aspx?classification=4894&code=O771200&action=expand

19 J.K. Gibson-Graham, J. Cameron and S. Healy, *Take Back the Economy* (Minnesota: University of Minnesota Press, 2013).

20 Ibid, 12.

21 Ibid, xx.

22 Te Puni Kōkiri, *Every Māori Counts*, 2012.

23 Hamer, *Maori In Australia*, 2007, 78.

24 Te Puni Kōkiri, *Every Māori Counts*, 2012.

25 W. LaDuke, 'Ware Lecture' (Unitarian Universalist General Assembly, 2010).

26 Ibid.

GLOSSARY

ahu whenua	a type of Māori land trust, governing Māori land
Aotearoa	one of the Māori names for New Zealand
hapū	sub-tribe
hui	a meeting
iwi	tribe
kapa haka	performing arts
karakia	prayer
kaumātua	elders
kaupapa Māori	issues pertaining to Māori
kawa	Māori procedures and protocols, usually pertaining to marae
koha	gift
mahi	work
marae	meeting place/ meeting house
Matatini	the National Kapa Haka Festival
moana	ocean
Ngāti Kahungunu	a Māori iwi located along the eastern coast of New Zealand's North Island
Ngāti Manawa	a Māori iwi located in Murupara and the central North Island region of New Zealand
Ngāti Porou	a Māori iwi located in the East Cape and Gisborne regions of the North Island of New Zealand
Ngāti Tūmatauenga	the New Zealand Army's Māori name
Pākehā	a New Zealander of European descent
ruku kaimoana	diving for seafood

rūnanga	tribal governance entity
tamariki	children
tauiwi	foreigner, non-Māori
Te Arawa	a Māori iwi located in Rotorua and the Bay of Plenty region of New Zealand's North Island
Te Ātiawa	a Māori iwi located in Wellington and Taranaki regions
te reo Māori	the Māori language
Te Tiriti o Waitangi	the Māori language version of the Treaty of Waitangi
Te Whānau-ā-Apanui	a Māori iwi located in the eastern Bay of Plenty and East Coast region of New Zealand's North Island
tikanga	Māori cultural practices
Tūmatauenga	the god of war
Tūwharetoa	a Māori iwi located in the central North Island of New Zealand
waka	boat
'Whakaaria Mai'	the hymn 'How Great Thou Art'
whakamā	embarrassed, shy
whakawhanaungatanga	fostering relationships with family
whānau	family
whenua	land

BIBLIOGRAPHY

INTERVIEWS CITED

John, 6 November 2013
MM, 19 September 2014
Nigel, 12 May 2013
Silver Surfer, 28 March 2013
Silver Surfer, 14 April 2013
Silver Surfer, 14 March 2014
T, 19 April 2013

BOOKS, ARTICLES, WEBSITES

Alexandra, A., D. Baker, and M. Caparini, eds. 2008. *Private Military Security Companies*. London: Routledge.
Anonymous Squadron Commander. 2003. 'Future Challenges to SOF in the Fight Against Global Terrorism.' Brief to PASOC, February 2003.
Ash, J. 2006. 'Yachting, a Safer life with the cup yachts.' *New Zealand Herald*, 24 June. http://www.nzherald.co.nz/sport/news/article.cfm?c_id=4&objectid=10388116 (accessed 19 June 2014).
Avant, D. 2006. *The Market for Force*. Cambridge: Cambridge University Press.
Bandow, D. (n.d). 'Privatizing Military Maintenance,' *CATO Institute*. http://www.cato.org/publications/commentary/privatizing-military-maintenance (accessed 25 January 2015).
Bearpark A., and S. Schulz. 2007. 'The Future of the Market.' In *From Mercenaries to Market: The Rise and Regulation of Private Military Companies*, edited by S. Chesterman and C. Lehnardt. Oxford: Oxford University Press.
Bello, W. 2004. *Deglobalization: Ideas for a New World Economy*. London: Zed Books.
BERL. 2010. *The Asset Base, Income and Expenditure and GDP of the 2010 Māori Economy*. Report to the Māori Economic Taskforce, Te Puni Kōkiri. http://www.tpk.govt.nz/en/in-print/our-publications/publications/the-asset-base-income-expenditure-and-gdp-of-the-2010/download/met-rep-assetbaseincexpend-2011.pdf (accessed 28 June 2015).

BERL. 2010. 'The Māori Economy: A Sleeping Giant?' 22 December. http://www.berl.co.nz/economic-insights/economic-development/Maori-economy/the-Maori-economy-a-sleeping-giant-about-to-awaken/ (accessed 28 December 2014).

BERL. 2010. 'The Māori Economy: Science and Innovation.' Report to the Māori Economic Taskforce. http://berl.co.nz/assets/Economic-Insights/Economic-Development/Maori-Economy/BERL-2011-Maori-Economy-Science-and-Innovation-Scenarios.pdf (accessed 6 January 2015).

Berndtsson, J. 2012. 'Security Professionals for Hire: Exploring the Many Faces of Private Security Expertise.' *Millennium: Journal of International Studies* 40 (2).

Bishop, R. 1998. 'Freeing Ourselves from Neo-Colonial Domination in Research: A Māori Approach to Creating Knowledge.' *Qualitative Studies in Education* 11 (2).

Blackwell, J.W. 2006. 'Private Military Companies: Their Emergence, Role and Impact on NZ Army Special Operations Personnel Turnover.' Unpublished dissertation; University of Leicester.

Bollard. A., and R. Barrow. 2012. 'Could we be better off than we think?' Speech to the Trans-Tasman Business Circle, Auckland. http://www.rbnz.govt.nz/research_and_publications/speeches/2012/4683869.pdf (accessed 23 January 2015).

Bourge, C. 2003. 'Analysis: Mercenary as Future Peacekeeper?' United Press International news.25August.http://www.upi.com/Business_News/Security-Industry/2003/08/25/Analysis-Mercenary-as-future-peacekeeper/24411061850942/ (accessed 25 January 2015).

Brooks, D., and M. Chorev. 2008. 'Ruthless humanitarianism: Why Marginalizing Private Peacekeeping Kills People.' In *Private military and security companies: Ethics, Policies and Civil-Military Relations*, edited by A. Alexandra, D. Baker and M. Caparini. London: Routledge.

Bryson, J., P. O'Neil and H. Lomax. 2008. 'Developing Human Capability: Employment Institutions, Organisations and Individuals: Māori Research Strand.' Discussion Paper. http://www.victoria.ac.nz/som/researchprojects/dhc-publtns/MāoriResearchStrandDiscussionPaper.pdf (accessed 28 December 2014).

Bush, G.W. 2001. Joint session of [U.S.] Congress, 20 September.

Carter, B. 2004. 'Dead Man Ignored Family's Pleas.' *New Zealand Herald*, 12 May. http:// www.nzherald.co.nz/nz/news/article.cfm?c_id=1&objectid=3565901 (accessed 19 June 2014).

Charman, P. 2013. 'Kiwi sees fighting off pirates as just a job.' *New Zealand Herald*, 20 July. http://www.nzherald.co.nz/nz/news/article.cfm?c_id=1&objectid=10900435 (accessed 6 January 2015).

Chatterjee. P. 2004. *Iraq, Inc. A Profitable Occupation*. New York: Seven Stories Press.

Chesterman, S., and C. Lehnardt, eds. 2007. *From Mercenaries to Market: The Rise and Regulation of Private Military Companies*. Oxford: Oxford University Press.

Chisholm, A. 2013. 'The Silenced and Indispensible.' *International Feminist Journal of Politics*. http://dx.doi.org/10.1080/14616742.2013.781441 (accessed 6 January 2015).

Chong Guan, K., and J.K. Skogan, eds. 2007. *Maritime Security in Southeast Asia*. New York: Routledge.

Clark, Helen. 2007. Speech presented at the NZDF No. 48 Command Staff Course.11 December. http://www.beehive.govt.nz/node/31606 (accessed 22 June 2014).

Clark, Helen. 2004. 'NZ Man Dies in Iraq.' Statement on 11 May 2004. http://www.beehive.govt.nz/node/19659 (accessed 19 June 2014).

Cleave, L. 2007. 'Kiwi in Iraq died doing work he loved.' *New Zealand Herald*, 13 July. http://www.nzherald.co.nz/nz/news/article.cfm?c_id=1&objectid=10451295 (accessed 22 June 2014).

Cockayne, J. 2007. 'Make or Buy? Principal-agent theory and the regulation of private military companies.' In *From Mercenaries to Market: The Rise and Regulation of Private military Companies*, edited by S. Chesterman and C. Lehnardt. Oxford: Oxford University Press.

Cody, J. F. 2012. *28th Māori Battalion*. Christchurch: Willson Scott Publishing Ltd.

Collins, Judith. 2004. 'Mercenary Activities (Prohibition) Bill: Second Reading.' *Hansard*, 29 June, http://www.parliament.nz/en-nz/pb/debates/debates/47HansD_20040701_00000249/mercenary-activities-prohibition-bill-%E2%80%94-second-reading (accessed 25 June 2014).

Cowan, J. 2011. *Māori in the Great War*. Christchurch: Willson Scott Publishing Ltd.

Cumming, G., and C. Masters. 2012. 'A Nation Divided: Inside the Urewera Four Trial.' *New Zealand Herald*, 24 March. http://www.nzherald.co.nz/nz/news/article.cfm?c_id=1&objectid=10794146 (accessed 6 January 2015).

Dearnaley, M. 2000. 'Ex-SAS shocked at condition of hostage tycoon.' *New Zealand Herald*, 10 March. http://www.nzherald.co.nz/nz/news/article.cfm?c_id=1&objectid=124961 (accessed 7 April 2014).

Dearnaley, M. 2000. 'Papers tell of diplomat's rescue slipup.' *New Zealand Herald*, 19 April. http://www.nzherald.co.nz/nz/news/article.cfm?c_id=1&objectid=132197 (accessed 28 June 2015).

Deskar, B. 2007. 'Re-thinking the safety of navigation in the Malacca Strait.' In *Maritime Security in Southeast Asia*, edited by K.C. Guan and J.K. Skogan. London: Routledge.

Dewes, H. 2005. 'Kiwis in Iraq Cut Adrift.' *Dominion Post*, 23 July.

Dua, J. 2013. 'A Pirate's Life for Me.' *New Internationalist*, September.

Eichler, M. 2014. 'Citizenship and the Contracting out of Military Work: From National Conscription to Globalized Recruitment.' *Citizenship Studies* 18.

Enloe, C. H. 1980. *Ethnic Soldiers: State Security in a Divided Society*. Middlesex: Penguin.

Erai, M.F. 1995. 'Māori Soldiers: Māori Experiences of the New Zealand Army.' MA thesis in Social Science Research. Victoria University of Wellington.

Feinstein, A. 2012. *The Shadow World: Inside the Global Arms Trade*. London: Penguin.

Ferrier Hodgson. 2002. 'Final Report to Creditors and Shareholders of Onix International Ltd.' 29 November. http://www.societies.govt.nz/scanned-images/05/BC10043185905.pdf (accessed 19 June 2014).

Field, M. 2013. 'NZ Part of NSA Surveillance – Snowden.' Stuff.co.*nz*, 1 August. http://www.stuff.co.nz/technology/8989755/NZ-part-of-NSA-surveillance-Snowden (accessed 19 June 2014).

Fifield, A. 2013. 'Contractors Reap $138bn from Iraq War.' *Financial Times*, 18 March. http://www.ft.com/cms/s/0/7f435f04-8c05-11e2-b001-00144feabdc0.html#axzz3LLPkRz95 (accessed 9 December 2014).

Finance and Expenditure Select Committee. 2003. 'Standard Estimates Questionnaire 2002/2003, Vote: Defence Force.'

Fisher, D. 2006. 'SAS Soldiers on $4.57 an Hour to Hunt Osama.' *New Zealand Herald*, Sunday, 30 April.
Gay, E. 2012. 'Security Expert Denies Telling Urewera Four How to Take Hostages.' *New Zealand Herald*, 7 March. http://www.nzherald.co.nz/nz/news/article.cfm?c_id=1&objectid=10790397 (accessed 6 January 2015).
George, S. 1999. *The Lugano Report: On Preserving Capitalism in the Twenty-First Century*. London: Pluto Press.
George, S. 2013. *Whose Crisis, Whose Future?* London: Polity Press.
Gibson-Graham, J.K. 2006. *A Postcapitalist Politics*. Minneapolis: University of Minnesota Press.
Gibson-Graham, J.K., J. Cameron, and S. Healy. 2013. *Take Back the Economy*. Minnesota: University of Minnesota Press.
Ginkel, B., and F. van der Putten, eds. 2010. *The International Response to Somali Piracy*. Leiden: Martinus Nijhoff Publishers.
Ginsburg, F. 2011. 'Native Intelligence: A Short History of Debates on Indigenous Media and Ethnographic Film.' In *Made to be Seen: Perspectives on the History of Visual Anthropology*, edited by M. Banks and J. Ruby. Chicago: University of Chicago Press.
Goff, Phil. 2003. 'Mercenary Activities (Prohibition) Bill: First Reading.' *Hansard*, 5 November. http://www.parliament.nz/en-nz/pb/debates/debates/47HansD_20031105_00001303/mercenary-activities-prohibition-bill-%E2%80%94-first-reading (accessed 25 June 2014).
Gorman, E. G. Scobie, and Y. Paek. 2013. 'Measuring Saving Rates in New Zealand: An Update.' Treasury Working Paper. http://www.treasury.govt.nz/publications/research-policy/wp/2013/13-04 (accessed 23 January 2015).
Greener, B. 2009. *The New International Policing*. London: Palgrave Macmillan.
Hager, N. 2011. *Other People's Wars: New Zealand in Afghanistan, Iraq and the War on Terror*. Nelson: Craig Potton Publishing.
Hamer, P. 2007. *Maori in Australia: Ngā Māori I Te Ao Moemoeā*. Wellington: Te Puni Kōkiri.
Haynes, M.G. 2011. 'LOGCAP Demystified: A Primer on LOGCAP Services.' *Army Sustainment: Professional Bulletin of United States Army Sustainment* 43 (6). http://www.alu.army.mil/alog/issues/NovDec11/LOGCAP_Demystified.html (accessed 17 December 2014).
Healy, H. 2013. 'Empire Strikes Back: Where Counter-Piracy is Going Wrong.' *New Internationalist*, September.
Hemara, R. 2013. 'Operation 8: Weaving the Police "Terrorism" Narrative.' *Te Putatara*. http://www.putatara.net/2013/11/op8-threads/ (accessed 6 January 2015).
Higate, P. 2012. 'Cowboys and Professionals: the Politics of Identity Work in the Private and Military Security Company.' *Millennium: Journal of International Studies* 40 (2).
Higate, P. 2012. 'In the Business of (In)Security? Mavericks, Mercenaries and Masculinities in the Private Security Company.' In *Making Gender, Making War: Violence and Peacekeeping Practices*, edited by A. Kronsell and E. Svedberg. New York: Routledge.
Higate, P. 2012. 'Martial Races and Enforcement Masculinities of the Global South: Weaponising Fijian, Chilean and Salvadoran Postcoloniality in the Mercenary Sector.' *Globalizations* 9 (1).

Hill, R. 2003. 'Introducing Policing into the Rangatiratanga Discourse: An Historical Overview of the Role of Māori Police Personnel.' In *Rangatiratanga Series 1*. Wellington: Treaty of Waitangi Research Unit.
Hokowhitu, B. 2004. 'Tackling Māori Masculinity: A Colonial Genealogy of Savagery and Sport.' *The Contemporary Pacific* 16 (2).
Huffington Post. 2012. 'Fact of the Day #8: US Defense Spending Dwarfs rest of World.' http://www.huffingtonpost.com/2012/08/06/defense-spending-fact-of-the-day_n_1746685.html (accessed 6 January 2015).
Human Rights Council. 2011. 'Draft of a possible Convention on Private Military and Security Companies (PMSCs) for consideration and action by the Human Rights Council.' http://psm.du.edu/media/documents/international_regulation/united_nations/human_rights_council_and_ga/open_ended_wg/session_1/un_open_ended_wg_session_1_draft-of-a-possible-convention.pdf (accessed 6 January 2015).
Irwin, K. 1994. 'Māori Research Methods and Practices.' *Sites* 28, Autumn.
Isenberg, D. 2012. 'The Rise of Private Military Security Companies.' *Somalia Report*, 26 May. http://www.somaliareport.com/index.php/post/3380/The_Rise_of_Private_Maritime_Security_Companies_ (accessed 21 December 2014).
Jager, T., and G. Kummel, eds. 2007. *Private Military Security Companies: Chances, Problems, Pitfalls and Prospects*. Wiesbaden: VS Verlag fur Sozialwissenschaften.
Kedgley, Sue. 2004. 'Mercenary Activities (Prohibition) Bill: Second Reading.' *Hansard*, 29 June. http://www.parliament.nz/en-nz/pb/debates/debates/daily/47HansD_20040701/volume-618-week-61-tuesday-29-june-2004continued-on (accessed 8 June 2014).
Kingi, T. 2013. 'Cultural Bastions, Farm Optimisation, and Tribal Agriculture in Aotearoa New Zealand.' Proceedings of the 22nd International Grasslands Conference.
Kinsey, C. 2007. 'Private Security Companies: Agents of democracy or Simply Mercenaries?' In *Private Military Security Companies: Chances, Problems, Pitfalls and Prospects*, edited by T. Jager and G. Kummel. Wiesbaden: VS Verlag fur Sozialwissenschaften.
Klein, N., J. Mossop, and DR Rothwell, eds. 2010. *Maritime Security: International Law and Policy Perspectives from Australia and New Zealand*. London: Routledge.
Kramer, D. 2007. 'Does History Repeat Itself? A Comparative Analysis of Private Military Entities.' In *Private Military Security Companies: Chances, Problems, Pitfalls and Prospects*, edited by T. Jager and G. Kummel. Wiesbaden: VS Verlag fur Sozialwissenschaften.
Krishnan, A. 2008. *War as Business: Technological Change and Military Service Contracting*. Hampshire: Ashgate.
Kukutai, T. and S. Pawar. 2013. 'A Socio-demographic Profile of Māori living in Australia.' NIDEA Working Paper no. 3, June. http://www.waikato.ac.nz/__data/assets/pdf_file/0006/156831/2013-WP3-A-Demographic-Profile-of-Maori-living-in-Australia.pdf (accessed 8 December 2014).
LaDuke, W. 2012. *The Militarization of Indian Country*. Michigan: Michigan State University Press.
LaDuke, W. 2010. 'Ware Lecture.' Presented at the Unitarian Universalist General Assembly. http://www.uua.org/ga/past/2010/ga2010/165861.shtml (accessed 25 January 2015).

Lilly, D. 2000. 'The Privatization of Peacekeeping: Prospects and Realities.' *Disarmament Forum: Peacekeeping Evolution or Extinction 3?* Geneva: United Nations.

Mac, K. 2009. 'NZ Contractors in Iraq.' *CONTACT Air, Land and Sea: The Australian Military Magazine* (15). http://www.contactairlandandsea.com/2009/story_packages/issue15/con15_kiwi_mac.pdf (accessed 21 December 2014).

Maclellan, N. 2006. 'From Fiji to Fallujah: The War in Iraq and the Privatisation of Private Security.' *Pacific Journalism Review* 12 (2).

Maggio, E. J. 2009. *Private Security in the 21st Century: Concepts and Applications.* Sudbury, Massachusetts: Jones and Bartlett Publishers.

Marcus, G. E. 1995. 'Ethnography in/of the World System: The Emergence of Multi-Sited Ethnography.' *Annual Review of Anthropology* 24.

Mark, Ron. 2003. 'Mercenary Activities (Prohibition) Bill: First Reading.' *Hansard*, November 5. http://www.parliament.nz/en-nz/pb/debates/debates/47HansD_20031105_00001303/mercenary-activities-prohibition-bill-%E2%80%94-first-reading (accessed 25 June 2014).

Mark, Ron. 2004. 'Second Reading of the Mercenary Activities (Prohibition) Bill.' *Hansard*, 29 June. http://www.parliament.nz/en-nz/pb/debates/debates/ daily/47HansD_20040701/volume-618-week-61-tuesday-29-june-2004continued-on (accessed 8 June 2014).

McNicholas, P., M. Humphries, and S. Gallhofer. 2004. 'Maintaining the Empire: Maori Women's Experiences in the Accountancy Profession.' *Critical Perspectives on Accounting* 15.

McPherson, M. 2007. 'Bay Security Guard Dies in Afghanistan War Zone.' *Bay of Plenty Times*, 15 December. http://www.nzherald.co.nz/bay-of-plenty-times/news/article.cfm?c_id=1503343&objectid=10964576 (accessed 6 January 2015).

Ministry of Business, Innovation and Employment. 2010. 'A Snapshot of the Māori Economy.' http://www.mbie.govt.nz/what-we-do/maori-economic-development/mefs.pdf (accessed 6 January 2015).

Ministry of Foreign Affairs and Trade. 2004. 'Mercenaries Activities (Prohibition) Bill: Report on Submissions.'

New Zealand Companies Office website, http://www.business.govt.nz/companies/app/ui/pages/companies/920127/shareholdings (accessed 28 June 2015).

New Zealand Defence Force. n.d. http://www.defencecareers.mil.nz/army/army-life/salaries-working-conditions (accessed 25 January 2015).

New Zealand Defence Force. 2013. 'Executive Overview of the New Zealand Defence Force.' http://www.nzdf.mil.nz/downloads/pdf/public-docs/2013/executive-overview-of-the-defence-force.pdf (accessed 8 December 2014).

New Zealand Defence Force. 2010. 'Part 9, Chapter 10: Paramilitary Employment.' *Defence Force Order 3: Human Resources Manual.* Wellington: New Zealand Defence Force.

New Zealand Defence Force. 2003. 'Annual Report For the Year Ended 30 June 2003.' Wellington: New Zealand Defence Force.

New Zealand Defence Force. 2003. 'NZDF Response to Foreign Affairs, Defence and Trade Select Committee Questionnaire,' 16 October.

New Zealand Herald. 2006. 'New Zealander Killed in Iraq Farwelled in Packed Ceremony.' *New Zealand Herald*, 21 August. http://www.nzherald.co.nz/nz/news/article.cfm?c_id=1&objectid=10397303 (accessed 27 December 2014).

New Zealand Herald. 2000. 'Mission: insoluble for Onix International.' *New Zealand Herald*, 18 December. http://www.nzherald.co.nz/nz/news/article.cfm?c_id=1&objectid=165585 (accessed 16 January 2015).

Office of the Commissioner for Human Rights, United Nations Human Rights Council, http://www.ohchr.org/EN/HRBodies/HRC/WGMilitary/Pages/OEIWGMilitaryIndex.aspx (accessed 28 June 2015)

Office for the Community and Voluntary Sector. 2007. *Mahi Aroha: Māori perspectives on volunteering and cultural obligations*. Wellington: Office for the Community and Voluntary Sector.

Ong-Webb, G. G., ed. 2006. *Piracy, Maritime Terrorism and Securing the Malacca Straits*. Singapore: Institute of South East Asian Studies.

Ortiz, C. 2007. 'The Private Military Company: An Entity at the Center of Overlapping Spheres of Commercial Activity and Responsibility.' In *Private Military Security Companies: Chances, Problems, Pitfalls and Prospects*, edited by T. Jager and G. Kummel. Wiesbaden: VS Verlag fur Sozialwissenschaften.

O'Rourke, S. 2006. 'Grief Shatters Family Haven.' *New Zealand Herald*, 11 August 2006. http://www.nzherald.co.nz/nz/news/article.cfm?c_id=1&objectid=10395665 (accessed 6 January 2015).

Pelton, R. Y. 2011. 'Somali Pirates Score Rich Returns When Ship Cargoes, Crews Are Left Intact.' Bloomberg News Service, 14 May. http://www.bloomberg.com/news/2011-05-13/somali-pirates-score-rich-returns-when-ship-cargoes-crews-are-left-intact.html (accessed 23 March 2014).

Radio New Zealand. 2006. 'Former NZ Soldier Reportedly Charged Over Lebanese Kidnapping.' 30 December. http://test.knowledge-basket.co.nz.helicon.vuw.ac.nz/databases/newztext-newspapers/view/?d8=rnz/text/2006/dec/30/1987ccd3.html (accessed 22 June 2014).

Rawlings, G. 1999. 'Villages, Islands and Tax Havens: The global/local implications of a financial entrepot in Vanuatu.' *Canberra Anthropology* 22 (2).

Richardson, M. 2004. *A Time Bomb for Global Trade: Maritime-related Terrorism in an Age of Weapons of Mass Destruction*. Singapore: Institute of Southeast Asian Studies.

Rona, G. 2013. 'Remarks.' Paper presented to the UN Working Group on the Use of Mercenaries, Montreux +5 Conference, 11–13 December. http://www.ohchr.org/EN/NewsEvents/Pages/DisplayNews.aspx?NewsID=14105&LangID=E (accessed 24 March 2014).

Sabin, B. 2012. 'Hostages Thank Kiwi Team for Pirate Rescue.' *TV3 News*, 27 February. http://www.3news.co.nz/world/hostages-thank-kiwi-team-for-pirate-rescue-2012022708#axzz3M6Nbumqq (accessed 6 January 2015).

Said, E. 1996. *Representations of the Intellectual*. New York: Vintage.

Scahill, J. 2013. *Dirty Wars: The World is a Battlefield*. London: Serpent's Tail.

Scahill, J. 2007. *Blackwater: The Rise of the World's Most Powerful Mercenary Army*. London: Serpent's Tail.

Scahill, J. 2007. 'War on Iraq.' 13 August. http://www.alternet.org/story/59571/flush_with_profits_from_the_iraq_war,_military_contractors_see_a_world_of_business_opportunities (accessed 9 April 2014).

Schwartz, M., J. Church. 2013. 'Department of Defense's Use of Contractors to Support Military Operations: Background Analysis and Issue for Congress.' Congressional

Research Service: Washington. http://www.fas.org/sgp/crs/natsec/R43074.pdf (accessed 6 January 2015).

Seed, J. 2014. 'Privatising the Hard Part: the New Zealand Experience of Employing Contractors to Deliver Military Logistic Support.' MA thesis, Victoria University of Wellington.

Sheehy, B., J. Maogoto, and V. Newell. 2009. *Legal Control of the Private Military Corporation*. Hampshire: Palgrave Macmillan.

Singer, Peter W. 2008. *Corporate Warriors: The Rise of the Privatized Military Industry*. 2nd ed. Ithaca: Cornell University.

Singer, Peter W. 2005. 'Outsourcing War.' *Foreign Affairs* 84 (2): 119–132.

Smith, L. T. 2008. 'Researching the Native in an Age of Uncertainty.' In *Handbook of Critical and Indigenous Methodologies*, edited by N. Denzin and Y. Lincoln. Los Angeles: Sage.

Smith, L. T. 1999. *Decolonizing Methodologies*. Otago: Otago University Press.

Smith, N. 2014. 'Bankrupt Kiwi Pirate-Fighters Operating Despite Owing Thousands.' *National Business Review*, 11 August.

Soutar, M. 2008. *Nga Tama Toa: The Price of Citizenship*. Wellington: David Bateman Ltd.

Southland Times. 2008. 'Junior doctors' pay increase won't keep them here.' *Southland Times*, 10 October. http://www.stuff.co.nz/southland-times/news/667836/Junior-doctors-pay-increase-will-not-keep-them-here (accessed 27 December 2014).

Spiller, C., L. Erakovic, M. Henare, and E. Pio. 2011. 'Relational Well-Being and Wealth: Māori Business and an Ethic of Care.' *Journal of Business Ethics* 98 (1).

Staff Reporters. 2000. 'Ex-SAS Men in Secret Rescue.' *New Zealand Herald*, 9 March. http://www.nzherald.co.nz/nz/news/article.cfm?c_id=1&objectid=124856 (accessed 6 January 2015).

Statistics New Zealand Classification Codes. http://www.stats.govt.nz/tools_and_services/ClassificationCodeFinder/ClassificationCodeHierarchy.aspx?classification=4894&code=O771200&action=expand (accessed 25 January 2015).

Stranger, A., and M.E. Williams. 2006. 'Private Military Corporations: Benefits and Costs of Outsourcing Security.' *Yale Journal of International Affairs*, Fall/Winter.

Swiss Federal Department of Foreign Affairs. 2008. 'The Montreux Document.' https://www.eda.admin.ch/eda/en/fdfa/foreign-policy/international-law/international-humanitarian-law/private-military-security-companies/montreux-document.html (accessed 22 December 2014).

Tahana, Y. 2012. 'Mozzies Buzzing in Rich Mining Territories.' *New Zealand Herald*, 23 June. http://www.nzherald.co.nz/nz/news/article.cfm?c_id=1&objectid=10814960 (accessed 6 January 2015).

Tapsell, P., and C. Woods. 2008. 'Pōtikitanga: Indigenous Entrepreneurship in a Māori Context.' *Journal of Enterprising Communities* 2 (3).

Te Ara Encyclopedia of New Zealand, 'Armed Forces', accessed 28 June 2015 http://www.teara.govt.nz/en/graph/35716/defence-force-personnel-by-gender-and-ethnicity-2012.

Te Puni Kōkiri. 2012. *He Kai Kei Aku Ringa: The Crown Māori Economic Growth Partnership*. Wellington: Te Puni Kōkiri.

Te Puni Kōkiri. 2012. *Every Māori Counts*. http://www.tpk.govt.nz/en/a-matou-mohiotanga/demographics/every-Māori-counts (accessed 6 January 2015).

Te Puni Kōkiri. 2011. *Māori Export Competitiveness*. Wellington: Te Puni Kōkiri.

Te Puni Kōkiri. 2011. *Māori Demographics for Economic Return*. http://www.tpk.govt.nz/en/a-matou-mohiotanga/business-and-economics/maori-demographics-for-economic-return/online/1 (accessed 19 January 2015).

Te Puni Kōkiri. 2010. *Lifting Māori Productivity*. Wellington: Te Puni Kōkiri.

Te Puni Kōkiri. 2008. *Kōkiri*. http://www.tpk.govt.nz/en/in-print/kokiri/kokiri-09-2008/our-warriors-of-the-land-sea-and-air-/ (accessed 6 January 2015).

The Guardian. 2010. 'US Contractors in Afghanistan and Iraq.' *The Guardian*, 16 August, http://www.theguardian.com/news/datablog/2010/aug/16/afghanistan-iraq-contractors-statistics (accessed 21 December 2014).

Tyner, J.A. 2006. *The Business of War: Workers, Warriors and Hostages in Occupied Iraq*. Aldershot: Ashgate.

United Nations. 1989. 'Procedural History of the International Convention against the Recruitment, Use, Financing and Training of Mercenaries General Assembly resolution 44/34.' New York, December 4. http://legal.un.org/avl/ha/icruftm/icruftm.html (accessed 25 June 2014)

United Nations Commission on Human Rights. 2005. 'The Use of Mercenaries as a Means of Violating Human Rights and Impeding the Exercise of the Right of Peoples to Self-determination.' http://www.unhcr.org/refworld/docid/45377c39c.html (accessed 1 October 2012).

United Nations General Assembly. 2012. 'United Nations Working Group on the use of mercenaries as a means of violating human rights and impeding the exercise of the right of people to self-determination.' Report to Sixty-seventh session,' August. http://daccess-dds-ny.un.org/doc/UNDOC/GEN/N12/476/27/PDF/N1247627.pdf?OpenElement (accessed 6 January 2015).

United Nations Human Rights Council. 2008. 'Mandate of the Working Group on the use of mercenaries as a means of violating human rights and impeding the exercise of the right of peoples to self-determination.' http://ap.ohchr.org/documents/E/HRC/resolutions/A_HRC_RES_7_21.pdf (accessed 1 October 2012).

US Commission on Wartime Contracting in Iraq and Afghanistan. 2011. 'Transforming Wartime Contracting: Final Report to Congress.' http://cybercemetery.unt.edu/archive/cwc/20110929214158/http://www.wartimecontracting.gov/docs/CWC_FinalReport-Ch1-lowres.pdf (accessed 21 December 2014).

Walker, F. 2012. 'Descendants of a Warrior Race: the Māori Contingent, the Pioneer Battalion and the Martial Race Myth 1914-1919.' *War and Society* 31 (1).

Wallwork, R. D. 2005. 'Operational Implications of Private Military Companies in the Global War on Terror.' Lecture to the School of Advanced Military Studies, United States Army Command and General Staff College, Fort Leavenworth, Kansas. http://www.dtic.mil/get-tr-doc/pdf?AD=ADA436294&Location=U2&doc=GetTRDoc.pdf (accessed 27 December 2014).

Waring, M. 1988. *If Women Counted*. San Franscico: Harper & Row.

Zamparini, L. 2014. 'Economic Issues in Maritime Transport Security.' In *Maritime Transport Security: Issues, Challenges and National Policies*, edited by K. Bichou, J.S. Szyliowicz, and L. Zamparini. Cheltenham: Edward Elgar.

INDEX

Tables are indicated in **bold**; figures and pictures in *italics*.

A

Abu Dhabi, 53
Afghanistan
   deaths of contractors in, 56
   NZ military in, 34, 36, 82
   'reset' of equipment in, 15
   SAS pay rates in, 29
   US invasion of, 3
   use of privatised military industry in, 9, 18, 43, 72
Africa
   east coast of, 36, 85, 92, 116, 119–20
   and Māori culture, 116–18
   map of, *32–3*
ahu whenua, 127
aid enablers, 19
AK-47s, 57, 75, 93
AKTS NZ LTD, 17
Al Qaeda, 85–6
Algeria, use of PMSCs in, 19
America's Cup, 33–4
Anadarko, 93
Anisi, Hemi, 35–6
Apiata, Willie, 35
APOD (Aerial Port of Debarkation), 50
ArmorGroup, 34, 42
arms industry, 4, 93–4
Australia, Māori living in, 4, 7, 34, 128, 135
Australians, in Iraq, 49, 58–9

B

Baghdad
   attacks in, 55–7, 63–4
   entries and exits of, 49–50, 73–4
   Shia in, 61–2
Bahrain, 91–2
bank accounts
   New Zealand, 76, 83
   offshore, 121
Barantas Security Group, 17, 91–2
BARS (Background Asia Risk Solutions), 103, 106–8
Basra, 47–8, 55, 61, 72, 75–6, 112, *116–7*
BIAP (Baghdad International Airport), 49, 56
bin Laden, Osama, 92
Blackwater/Xe/Academi, 42, 54, 103
Blackwell, Jim, 14
Blake, Peter, 33–4
bodyguards, 129
Bosnia, MPRI in, 3
Bougainville, 23
bouncers, 129

British Army
  and East India Company, 10
  former members in PMSCs, 12
  in Iraq, 48–9, 55, 59, 63, 76–7
  outsourcing logistics, 72
British Government, protecting employees of, 51
Brize Norton, 50
Brunei, 47, 86
business experience, 98–9, 135–7

C
cable laying, 81, 85
Cambodia, 44–7, 64–5, 125
Cheney, Dick, 72
cigarettes, cartons of, 90
Clark, Helen, 29, 35, 112
coffins, 55–6
Collins, Judith, 25
Colombia, 54
combat logistics, 71
communal lifestyle, 62, 134
connections, 47–8, 59, 63
contractor wars, 9
corporatisation, 12
CRG (Control Risk Group), 47, 103

D
de Thierry, Darryl, 34, 36
defence sector, Māori working in, 129, **130**
Department of Corrections (NZ), 129
diverse economy, 127, 131, 132, 135, 137
DynCorp International, 42, 72

E
economic and military power, 9–10
economic roles, multiple, 132
Egypt, 90
EMSS (Energy and Maritime Security Services), 17, 91

Envoy 360, 17, 82, 92–3
Erbil, 50–3
ERG Partners, 103
ethnic groups
  in military forces, 10, 137
  as PMSCs in Iraq, 42–3
export orientation, 126
extractive industries, 125

F
Fallujah, 49
Fijians, 10, 57–8, 62
Flour Intercontinental, 72
forward logistics, 71
Franks, Stephen, 25

G
GDP (gross domestic product), 126, 128
Germany, 88–9
Gibraltar Strait, 89–90
Goff, Phil, 23
gold mining, 115–16, 121
Green Zone, Baghdad, 55–6, 61–2, 73–4, 112
Gulf of Aden, 82, 87, 109, 120
Gulf War (1991), 15, 42
Gurkhas, 10, 73

H
haka, 60, 113–14
Halliburton, 42, 72
Hamer, Paul, 135
Hanoi, 44
hapū
  contact with, 125
  contributing to, 79, 131–3
  political strength of, 4
Hart Security, 83, 86, 88, 91, 107–10
Hartono, Roesli, 33
Hauraki, Anthony, 33

He Toki Huna (film), 36
Hislop, Nathan, 34
Hodeidah, 93
Hong Kong, 53, 103
hostages, rescuing, 91
human rights, 16, 19
Hunt, Rau, 35

I

ICoC (International Code of Conduct for Private Security Service Providers), 17–18
impunity, 14
Indonesia, Onix operation in, 3, 33–4
infrastructure, protecting, 41
Inland Revenue Department (IRD), 30, 121
international organisations, use of PMSCs, 18–19
International Strategic Development Solutions, 36
investment enablers, 19
Iraq
  deaths of contractors in, 56
  entry and exit points, 49–50, 52
  military equipment in, 15, 57–8
  New Zealanders in security work in, 25, 27, 34–6, 78, 111–12
  US invasion of, 3, 41
  US withdrawal from, 109
  use of privatised military industry in, 9, 15, 18, 41–4, 71–2
  wages for security work in, 54, 65, 115
ISPS (International Port and Ship Security Code), 86
iwi
  feeling close to, 79
  governance entities of, 127
  supporting initiatives of, 131–2, 137
IZ, *see* Green Zone

K

Karachi, 92
karakia, 113, 117
kaupapa Māori, 6
KBR (Kellogg, Brown and Root), 42, 72, 82
Kennedy, Alpha, 36
Kenya, 10, 88, 92, 116, 118–20
Khmer Rouge (KR), 45–6
Kirkuk, 50, 52, 111
Kroll, 103
Kukutai, Tahu, 128
Kurds, 52
Al-Kut, 51, 63
Kuwait, 49–50, 65, 77, 79

L

LaDuke, Winona, 137
languages, 62, 115–16
Lebanon, Pemberton kidnapping in, 34
lethal force, 10, 14, 41, 119
LNs (local nationals), 42, 44, 56, 119
Locke, Keith, 26–7
Lockheed Martin, 15
LOGCAP (Logistics Civil Augmentation Program), 71–2
logistics, 41–2, 71–2, 77–8, 99

M

Malacca Straits, 82, 103
Māori
  in Afghanistan, 59
  in Africa, 120–1
  definitions of being, 128
  in Iraq, 47–8, 58–9, 62–3, 72–6, 111, 114–16
  living overseas, 128, 135
  as martial race, 11
  in media reports on PMSCs, 3, 33–6

Māori *(Continued...)*
  opposition to oil exploration, 93
  role in privatised military industry, 3-7, 35, 129, *131*, 132
  seen as New Zealanders, 43, 58
Māori businesses, 126, 128
Māori cultural economy, 134
Māori culture, and PMSC work, 59-60, 62, 79, 113-18
Māori economy
  global diversity of, 132, 137-8
  marginalised communities in, 4-5
  PMSC contribution to, 132-5
  scope of, 125-8
Māori land, 4, 79, 126-8, 135
Māori language (te reo), 114, 116
Māori sovereignty, 35
marae
  helping out on, 60, 133-4
  management of, 127
maritime security, *116-7*
  deaths in, 122
  government support in, 120
  Māori working in, 35-6, 83, 104, 118, 120-1
  use of term, 81
  vessels used in, 109
maritime trade routes, 81-2
Mark, Ron, 25-6
martial races, 10-11
Matrix Security, 93
mercenaries
  defined in NZ law, 24-6
  and PMFs/PMSCs, 9, 13, 16
  UN convention on, *see* UN (United Nations), Mercenary Convention
Mercenary Activities (Prohibition) Bill, 23-6, 28, 30
middle class, 133
Middle East, map of, *32-3*

military consulting firms, 41
military hardware
  high-tech, 12
  modified, 58
  PMSCs selling to states, 15
military provider firms, 41
military support firms, 41
Mombasa, 5, 91, *116-7*
Montreux Document on Pertinent International Legal Obligations and Good Practices for States related to Operations of Private Military and Security Companies during Armed Conflict, 18
Mosul, 51-3
MPRI (Military Professionals Resources Incorporated), 3, 42
MSS (Maritime Security Specialists), 106-8
multinational teams, fitting into, 43
Muscat, *116-7*

N
Nasiriyah, 50-1
Native Americans, 137
natural resources, 46-7, 65; *see also* extractive industries
NavSec International Limited, 17
Near East Security Services, 18
neo-liberalism, 11-12, 126
New Zealand
  economic contribution of PMSCs, 132-3
  maritime security in, 93
  PMSC work available in, 33-4
  regulation of PMSCs in, 23-6, 28
New Zealand 2013 Census, 129
New Zealand Army Special Operations unit, 43
New Zealand Consulate in Kuwait, 79
New Zealand Herald, 33, 35

New Zealand Police, 129
New Zealand Wars, 11
New Zealanders
  business skills of, 102
  employed by PMSCs, 30
  expatriate, 128, 135
  global reputation of, 43, 59–61, 92, 115–16
  in Iraq, 34–6, 48, 74–5, 77–8, 114–15
  in maritime security work, 83–4, 104–6, 118–19
  and tikanga Māori, 114
Ngamata, Teina, 34
Ngata, Apirana, 11
Ngāti Manawa, 98, 110
NGOs, and PMSCs, 16, 18–19
Nishtun, 85
non-observed economy, 127–8
NZDF (New Zealand Defence Force)
  differences from private sector, 77–8, 98
  employing Māori, 5, 128, 129
  former members in PMSCs, 25–8, 72, 82–3, 97, 103, 111
  retention of personnel, 28–30
  role of Māori culture in, 11, 117
  salaries in, 5
NZSAS (New Zealand Special Air Service), 101, 108

O

offshore logistics, 110
offshore security companies, 121
oil industry
  in Iraq, 51
  maritime protection for, 91, 93, 103–4
  and privatised military industry, 4, 19
oil trading, 110
Oman, 116-7

maritime security in, 87
Ron Mark working in PMSC in, 25
Onix International, 3, 33–4
Operation 8, 35

P

Pacific Islanders, 133, 135
Pakistan
  maritime security in, 91–2
  TCNs from, 43, 62
Papua New Guinea, 23
Pemberton, David, 34
Phnom Penh, 45
piracy, 81, 85, 91, 94, 120
PMFs (privatised military firms), 13, 27
PMSCs (Private Military and Security Companies)
  categories of, 41
  conflict with workers, 105–6
  dominance of large, 82
  escorting arms shipments, 93–4
  identity and reputation of, 13–15, 19, 91
  Māori as owners and managers of, 33, 53, 97, 111
  relationship with military, 76–7
  setting up, 102–4, 108
porcupine profile, 57
Port Sultan Qaboos, 116-7
Portugal, 89
primary industries, Māori economy and, 127
privatisation, 12, 42, 71, 148
privatised military industry
  absence of hierarchy in, 78, 83
  clients of, 12, 18–19
  deaths and injuries in, 34–5, 56
  ethnicity in, 10
  expansion of, 3, 11
  explaining to outsiders, 65–8
  incomes in, 5, 29, 53–5, 82–3

privatised military industry
  (*Continued...*)
  international regulation of, 16–18
  job security in, 112
  lack of backup in, 63–4
  in Māori economy, 3, 5, 128, 129, 131, 137
  New Zealanders' overseas earnings from, 30, 78, 83, 129
  recruitment in, 42–4, 47–9, 72, 102
productivity, 126
Provision, 93
pseudonyms, 6

R
Ramadi, 49
rear logistics, 71
Red Key Security, 27
religious faith, 108
remittance payments, 135
renewable energy, 137
'reset,' 15
Rewi, Michael, 34
Rhino, 73
Rice, Barrie, 34–5
Romanians, 63–4
Royal New Zealand Navy, 82; see also NZDF
rugby
  in Basra, 75
  in Cambodia, 47, 65, 125
  Fijians playing, 58
  as metaphor, 110
  in Singapore, 97–8
Rumsfeld, Donald, 71
rūnanga, 47, 136

S
Saddam Hussein, 41, 111, 113
Sadoun Street, Baghdad, 66–7
al-Sadr, Muqtada, 50, 61

Sadr City, Baghdad, 62
Salalah, 87
Samoans, 58, 83
Sana'a, 83–6, 88, 93
Sandline Affair, 23
SAS (Special Air Services), 27–9, 33, 84, 107
security breaches, 30
security guards, 93, 129
security sector, Māori working in, 129, **130**
Shaibah Log Base, 75
Shia Muslims, 51–2, 61–2
Singapore
  SARS outbreak in, 101
  training courses in, 86–7
Singapore Rugby Union (SRU), 97–8
al-Sistani, Ali, 61
smuggling, 94
Soldiers of Fortune (documentary), 35
Somalia
  piracy off coast of, 91, 94
  PMSCs in, 18
SOPs (standard operating procedures), 104
Southeast Asia
  map of, *32–3*
  maritime security in, 105
special forces, former members of, 27–30, 42–4, 48–9, 115
Special Tactics Group, 27
Spicer, Tim, 23
Suez Canal, 90–1
suicide bombings, 61, 66–7
Sunni Muslims, 51–2, 61–2
survey ships, 85, 87
Swords of Qadisiyah, 111, *116–7*

T
Tamihere, John, 3, 33
tangi, 79, 86, 131, 133

Tanzania, 44, 91, 115–18, 120
taxation
    avoiding, 53, 112, 135
    and offshore accounts, 121
    paying in New Zealand, 30, 76, 83, 133
    and vertical integration, 15
TCNs (third-country nationals), 42–4, 54, 56
Te Tiriti o Waitangi/Treaty of Waitangi, 126–7
Te Whānau-ā-Apanui, 93
Te Whenua Māori Act/the Māori Land Act 1993, 126
team leaders, 67, 83–8, 118
TEES, 102
Thai Maritime Solutions Co, 18
Thailand, 97
tikanga Māori, *see* Māori culture
training courses, 86–7, 102
transnational corporations, 4, 12, 16, 18–19
Triple Canopy, 42, 103
Trojan Global Protection, 18
Tūwharetoa, 117
Tyrrell, John Robert, 35

U
UN (United Nations)
    arms embargoes, 94
    in Cambodia, 45
    Convention on the Oceans and Law of the Sea, 81
    Mercenary Convention, 16–17, 23–4, 26
    and PMSCs, 3
United States military
    compensation paid to victims of, 14, 82
    identity cards, 77
    use of PMSCs, 15–16, 18, 42–3
Unity Resources Group, 103
US State Department, 77

V
Valour Security, 17
vertical integration, 14–15
Vessel Offshore Management, 88–9
volunteer work, 127, 131, 133

W
waiata, 60, 113, 117
Waipareira Trust, 3, 33
war zones, 4, 46, 114–15
weapons
    in maritime security, 87–8, 119–20
    permission to carry, 77, 93
    training with, 75
Westland Ltd, 33
'Whakaaria Mai,' 117
whakamā, 114
whakawhanaungatanga, 134
whānau, 4, 6, 60, 113, 117, 132–5
Whatuira, Ken, 3, 33
women
    in PMSCs, 77
    work of, 128
world map, political, *32–3*

Y
Yemen, *116-7*
    maritime security in, 83–4, 86–8, 93, 109
Yugoslavia, former, 11

Z
Zakho, 49, 52